English:
The Basic Skills

Imelda Pilgrim

John Nield

Nelson Thornes

Text © Imelda Pilgrim, John Nield 2008

Original illustrations © Nelson Thornes Ltd 2008

The right of Imelda Pilgrim and John Nield to be identified as authors of this work has been asserted by them in accordance with the Copyright, Designs and Patents Act 1988.

All rights reserved. No part of this publication may be reproduced or transmitted in any form or by any means, electronic or mechanical, including photocopy, recording or any information storage and retrieval system, without permission in writing from the publisher or under licence from the Copyright Licensing Agency Limited, of Saffron House, 6-10 Kirby Street, London, EC1N 8TS.

Any person who commits any unauthorised act in relation to this publication may be liable to criminal prosecution and civil claims for damages.

Published in 2009 by:
Nelson Thornes Ltd
Delta Place
27 Bath Road
CHELTENHAM
GL53 7TH
United Kingdom

09 10 11 12 13 / 10 9 8 7 6 5 4 3 2 1

A catalogue record for this book is available from the British Library

ISBN 978 1 4085 0552 61

Cover photograph © Nelson Thornes Ltd

Illustrations by Tom Cole of Seamonsterdesign.co.uk and Marcus Perry

Page make-up by Pantek Arts Ltd

Printed and bound in Spain by Graphycems

Contents

	Introduction	4
1	All about me	6
2	Make words work	10
3	Sentence sense	14
4	Building paragraphs	18
5	Planning control	22
6	Correcting correctly	26
7	Story time	30
8	Taking a break	34
9	Finding information	38
10	Finding the right answer	42
11	Meet and eat	46
12	Phones at work	50
13	Writing a report	54
14	A sporting chance	58
15	Read, respond, go	62
16	Organising your day	66
17	Safety first	70
18	Get to the point	74
19	Virtual writing	78
20	Face to face	82
21	Presentation matters	86
22	Building reports	90
23	Communicating persuasively	96
24	Complex and clear	102
25	Persuasive powers	106
26	Wild thoughts	110
27	Improving your writing	114
28	Why wear fur?	118

Punctuation

1	Punctuation basics	124
2	Commas	126
3	Apostrophes	128
4	Inverted commas	130

Spelling

1	Syllables	132
2	Suffixes and prefixes	133
3	Plurals	136
4	Homonyms	137
5	Using a dictionary	138

Acknowledgements   140

Introduction

Communication skills

People do all kinds of work, have all sorts of families, and participate in a wide range of leisure activities. Communication plays a vital part in all these aspects of life. To function successfully, you need to have command of good communication skills. Put simply, these skills are reading, writing, and speaking and listening. Achieving a qualification in Functional English will show that you have mastered the basic skills necessary in all three areas.

How this book helps

The texts and activities in this book are chosen to help you develop these skills and pass your Functional English tests and assessments.

Reading

There are all sorts of different texts in this book. Reading the texts closely and working through the structured activities will help you to become a more sophisticated reader who not only understands the detail and implications of a text, but is also able to respond appropriately and use texts to gather information.

Writing

The writing tasks provide detailed guidance on how to communicate information, ideas and opinions effectively and persuasively in a range of written forms. The spelling and punctuation sections at the end of the book will help you to ensure that your writing is clear and accurate.

Speaking and Listening

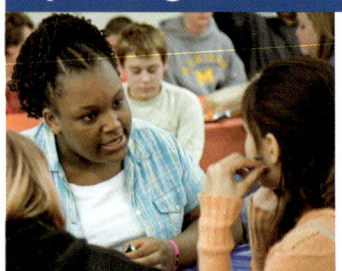

The speaking and listening tasks give you the opportunity to take part in a range of discussions and to make individual presentations, helping you to express your ideas clearly and effectively and listen carefully to what others say.

INTRODUCTION

Assessing your learning

Throughout each unit there are opportunities for you to check your learning, either on your own or with other students. This is your chance to review and assess your work, keep track of your learning, and set personal targets.

We hope you enjoy the texts and activities in this book and that by working carefully through the units you develop your skills and confidence in reading, writing, and speaking and listening.

Reading, writing, and speaking and listening skills are important in all kinds of situations.

5

1 All about me

In this unit ...
you will learn how to write a personal profile for a website, making sure that your work is clear and includes an appropriate level of detail for the audience and purpose.

There are many international websites, such as MySpace and Facebook, where people can enter their profiles and view friends' profiles. You must be a member yourself in order to access other people's profiles.

Warning! Never give your address to someone you have met on the internet, or arrange to meet them alone. If you are under 16, do not arrange to meet someone you have met on the internet without first talking to your parents or guardian.

Giving basic information

The first thing you are often asked to give is basic information about yourself. Most of this is very straightforward. Occasionally you are given drop-down boxes from which you should make a choice, like the ones shown on the right.

1 Below is a printed version of a web page, listing the kind of information you may need to provide. Make a list of the details you would give about yourself.

- Gender
- Date of birth (month, day and year)
- Occupation
- County
- Country
- Height
- I am here for:
  - dating
  - serious relationships
  - friends
  - networking

1 All about me

Giving more information

Once you have completed the basic details, you may be asked to give more information about yourself. Your aim is to be clear, informative and concise. Aim to keep each entry to fewer than fifty words.

2
- a Read all the sub-headings listed below.
- b Make notes on what you could write under each sub-heading.
- c Highlight the details most likely to interest the kind of reader you want to make contact with.
- d Write your profile.

Profile: interests and personality

- About me
- I'd like to meet
- Interests
- Music
- Movies
- Television
- Books
- Heroes

Checkpoint

When you have completed your profile, show it to two or three other students you know well. Ask them:
- what would make them want to contact you
- what improvements they think you could make.

Consider their comments carefully and make any changes you think would be helpful.

English: The Basic Skills

Writing a CV

When you apply for college, university or for a job, you need to give a more formal account of yourself. Many course organisers or employers will ask you to complete a CV, which stands for curriculum vitae, or life story. They do not want the full story of your life, though. They want you to:

- pick out the details that might be relevant to the course or job
- tell them something about the kind of person you are.

Your CV will be mainly to do with your education, work experience and interests.

The following CV was written in application for an administrative post with a local council. Read the CV and the annotations that accompany it carefully. You are going to use this as a model to write parts of your own CV.

Start with a general statement highlighting qualities appropriate to the post.

Then list basic information.

Next, give details of education.

List any work experience you have, giving the most recent first.

Outline your main interests to give a sense of the kind of person you are.

Give details of any skills that are relevant to the application.

Always give two referees. These may be for work-related, academic or character references. Always ask your referees for their permission first.

CURRICULUM VITAE

I am prepared to work hard and am reliable, flexible and helpful. I adapt readily to different situations and learn quickly. I hope you will give me the opportunity to work for you.

PERSONAL DETAILS
Name: Lucy Barnes
Date of birth: 13th June 1991
Address: 19 Holliers Place, York, YO28 8FS
Tel. no.: 07853 422538
E-mail: silver_star124@fastmail.com

EDUCATION
2005-2007 (York College): GCSEs: English (C), English Literature (B), Maths (D), Media Studies (C), Drama (A), ICT (B), French (B)

WORK EXPERIENCE
2007 to present: Part-time Sales Assistant, The Theatre Suppliers, Silver Street, York

INTERESTS
I enjoy travel and have been to Europe several times, including a placement with a French family. I have pursued an interest in dance and drama from childhood, and have taken part in a number of concerts and pantomimes. This has involved working with adults and other young people and has taught me the importance of being reliable and consistent and working hard in order to be successful.

SKILLS
I am an organised person who plans ahead and gives full attention and effort to the task in hand. I enjoy working co-operatively with other people as part of a team and believe I contribute positively whilst also learning a great deal. I am comfortable in the use of a range of ICT skills, such as word processing and SPSS.

REFERENCES
Mrs J. Clifford, 76 Acomb Road, Newcastle NE3 2BS

Ms S. Lee, York College, Tadcaster Road, York, YO24 1UA (Teacher)

1 **All about me**

3 You are now going to write part of your own CV. Use the CV on page 8 as a model.

   a First, think of a holiday job you might be interested in applying for. Below are some examples, but you could choose your own:

   sales assistant   office clerk   care assistant

   farm worker   holiday camp worker

   b List the qualities you think would be needed for the job you have chosen.

   c Using your list, write an opening statement showing how your personality matches the qualities that would be needed for the job.

4 Now make notes of what you would include under each of the six sub-headings: 'Personal details', 'Education', 'Work Experience', 'Interests', 'Skills' and 'References'.

5 Write the entries you would make for 'Interests' and 'Skills'. Aim to write between 50 and 100 words for each.

Checkpoint

When you have completed your entries for 'Interests' and 'Skills', show them to two or three other students.

Find out their answers to the following questions, and their reasons for their answers.

- What impression is made by the interests you have detailed?
- Do your skills make you seem a suitable applicant for the job you have applied for?
- If they were the employer, would they call you to interview?.

What improvements do they think you could make? Consider their comments carefully and make any changes you think would be helpful.

Throughout your working life, you will need to update your CV and adapt it to the different posts you apply for.

Summary

In this unit you have:
- given basic information for an informal website
- created a website profile
- learned about how to construct a CV
- completed the interests and skills sections of a CV.

2 Make words work

In this unit ...

you will look at how speech is used in different situations. You will also consider the differences between formal and informal speech.

We speak in many different ways. Look at and read the following cartoon sketches showing two informal situations. What do you notice about the differences in the ways the boy speaks? Suggest reasons for these differences.

I'll be back as soon as I can. I've got football. When I get back I'll tell you all about it 'n' we'll have our own knock about. Wish me luck.

Hey Mum, don't forget ... footy t'night. I'll be late. Back about six.

Identifying purpose and audience

The way we speak and the words we use usually depend on our purpose and audience.

The **purpose** is our reason for speaking.

The **audience** is the person or people we are speaking to.

Every day we speak in a range of situations. Usually we adapt what we say and how we say it to our audience and purpose.

Pair activity

1. In each of the following sketches the student, John, has yet to speak. Working in pairs, discuss with your partner:
   a the purpose and audience of what John will say
   b the different things he might say in each situation.

2. Look back at the first two sketches above. Explain in writing how the different audiences would affect the way the boy speaks.

What did you do at the weekend?

You're more than ten minutes late...where have you been?

I want to find out students' views on uniform. Tell me what you think.

Hiya. Good day?

10

2 Make words work

Group activity

3 Think about the following two situations:
   a explaining to a friend why you want to drop a particular subject.
   b explaining to a teacher why you want to drop a particular subject.

   Work in a group of three. One of you is going to speak in the role of **a**. The second is going to speak in the role of **b**. The third is going to listen carefully to both and report back the differences in:
   - what is said
   - how it is said.

   As a group list at least three reasons that would explain the differences you have noticed.

Choosing words carefully

What you say and the way you say it has a direct impact on the person you are speaking to.

4 a What are the differences in the ways the pupil handles a difficult situation in the pictures below?

   Imagine you are the teacher.
   b What would you think about:
   - the student in sketch 1
   - the student in sketch 2
   - the student in sketch 3?

   c What different things would you say to the student in these situations?

1 "Miss, could I have a minute? I haven't done my homework, Miss. I'm really sorry. Could I hand it in tomorrow morning?"

2 "Oh Miss, I forgot to do it. I'm sorry. I will do it."

3 "I haven't got it. I didn't know we had homework!"

11

English: The Basic Skills

Speaking formally and informally

The way we speak often depends on how well we know the person or people we are talking to. Many of the situations in which we speak are informal. The language we use reflects this. We might, for example, speak in local dialect or use slang or shortened words.

> I ain't goin'. I'd've liked to … but we've gotta go 'n' see Nanna on Sunday, 'cause it's her birthday.

There are times, however, when we need to speak in a more formal way and use standard English. Standard English is the way the language is spoken in more formal situations.

Pair activity

5 The following sentences contain non-standard English. In pairs, work out which words and phrases are non-standard. For each one, decide on an appropriate standard form that could be used in more formal situations and write it down.

a He couldn't of done it.
b We was just going there.
c I'm gonna get my work done before I go out.
d Look at them cars over there.
e Oh yeah … be there in a mo.
f The lights were kinda cool.

Using language to influence

Most people use language in a certain way to create a certain impression of themselves. Knowing when and how to vary the way you speak gives you the power to influence the way others respond to you.

Connexions provides information, advice, guidance and access to personal development opportunities for young people.

Connexions' personal advisers, including those based in schools and colleges, can give young people a wide range of advice. First they need to find out more about each person. This is sometimes done in an interview.

Group activity

6 You are going to carry out a trial interview. Work in groups of three. Decide which of you is person A, B and C.
- **A** will be the Connexions personal adviser
- **B** will be the interviewee
- **C** will be the observer.

Now read the following points and plan for the interview. Think about how the interview would start. The personal adviser would want to make the student feel comfortable and explain the reason for the interview. On the next page are the types of question the personal adviser might ask.

2 Make words work

- Let's start with now. How are you doing in school/college?
- What subjects do you like/not like?
- What do you like doing in your spare time and why?
- What job would you like to do when you leave school/college?
- Have you talked this over at home?
- Tell me what you think this job would involve.
- What do you think you would be good at in this job?
- What do you think you might find difficult about it?
- What do you think your employer might be looking for?

A Personal adviser
You will need to keep brief notes and may need to ask more questions.

B Interviewee
You need to think about the answers you can give. If the interview is to be helpful, you need to give as much detail as you can. As this is a formal situation, you should speak in standard English.

C Observer
At the end of the interview, you are going to comment on both the personal adviser and the interviewee. You need to focus on:
- how helpful the personal adviser is to the interviewee
- how the interviewee responds and the impression he or she creates.

Now carry out the interview.

Checkpoint

Read the following and then take turns to report back to your group.

A Personal adviser Say what you found out about the interviewee. Were there questions you would have liked more detailed answers to? Did the interviewee use language appropriately? What impression did you form of the interviewee? If you were to do the interview again, what changes would you make?

B Interviewee Say how you felt the interview went. Did you get the chance to say what you wanted to? Did you use language appropriately? What kind of impression do you think you made? If you were to do the interview again, what changes would you make?

C Observer Say, with reasons, whether you thought the personal adviser was helpful. Report on what you observed about the way the interviewee responded to the questions. Did they both use language appropriately? What suggestions for change would you make if the interview were to be done again?

Summary

In this unit you have:
- learned how speech varies to suit purpose and audience
- recognised the difference between informal and formal speech
- found out how to use speech to influence others.

3 Sentence sense

In this unit …
you will learn about simple, compound and complex sentences and how to use them. You will learn to make your writing suitable for different readers. You will also learn how to punctuate sentences correctly.

A sentence is a group of words that make complete sense.

Pair activity

1 With a partner, decide which of the following are not sentences. Explain why not.
a The boy, having seen the teacher, walked slowly towards him.
b Where the reddest strawberries grow.
c I walked to the local shop and found everything I wanted.
d The shop assistant, having noticed the customer outside.
e Although he was late.

Sentence structures

There are three main types of sentence structure: simple, compound and complex.

A **simple sentence** is the first kind of sentence you learn to write. It consists of one main clause, which makes complete sense on its own. For example:

The bus was late. We walked home.
  main clause   *main clause*

A **compound sentence** has two or more main clauses joined by *and*, *or*, *but* or *so*. These joining words are called conjunctions. For example:

The bus was late so we walked home.
                    conjunction
main clause   *main clause*

A **complex sentence** has a main clause and one or more subordinate clauses. A subordinate clause does not make complete sense on its own. For example:

Having realised the bus was late, we walked home.
      subordinate clause   *main clause*

2 a Identify each of the sentences below as simple, compound or complex. Look at the definitions above if you are not sure.

The man, who was only about twenty, walked in with an air of confidence.
He walked towards the reception but then he seemed to change his mind.
He stopped abruptly.
Glancing at his watch, he hurried away in the opposite direction.

b Copy and annotate each one to show the main clauses, conjunction and subordinate clauses.

3 Use conjunctions to form compound sentences by combining two or more of the simple sentences at the top of page 15.

3 Sentence sense

Some simple conjunctions
and
or
but
so

The shopping centre was crowded.
The young couple went for a coffee.
There was a long queue.
They joined it.
A little girl was crying.
The security man spoke to her.

4 Copy the following complex sentences. Highlight the main clause in one colour and the subordinate clause(s) in another colour.

Kellogg, the global breakfast cereal company, has been selling some of its most famous brands in Britain with higher salt and sugar levels than in its native US.

On British shelves, the Kellogg's high-fibre *All Bran* contains 138 per cent more salt than in the US, while the spin-off *All Bran Yoghurt* has 117 per cent more sugar.

Britons breakfasting on *Special K*, promoted as the healthy way to start the day, are munching 31 per cent more sugar.

(The Independent 25 October 2006)

5 With a partner, read the extracts below. Decide whether each sentence used is:
- simple
- compound
- complex.

Jane and Jack love the seaside. They go there for their holidays. They like to play on the sand or sometimes they swim in the sea. They are both good swimmers. The sea is often very cold but they don't mind. They have big, warm towels. Sometimes their Daddy takes them to the rock-pools. They take their nets and look for little fish. The fish usually escape.

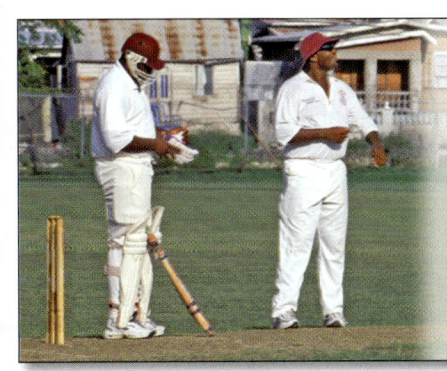

Once a British colony and nicknamed 'Little England', Barbados can appear very British with afternoon teas and starched school uniforms. One 19th-century visitor declared it 'more English than England itself'. There is a Hastings, a Brighton and a Worthing, all names of English towns, and a Trafalgar Square in Bridgetown, the island's capital. The game of cricket is practically the national religion.

Insight Guide: Caribbean – The Lesser Antilles

6 Writers vary the way they write to suit their intended audience.
   a What have you noticed about:
   - the range of sentences used in the first text
   - the range of sentences used in the second text?
   b Suggest reasons for the difference in the range of sentence structures in the two texts.

English: The Basic Skills

Checkpoint

Continue the story about Jane and Jack, which is written for young children. Use only simple and compound sentences. Aim to write between eight and ten sentences.

Swap your writing with another student. Make sure it is written in simple and compound sentences only.

Making writing interesting

When we first learn to read and write we almost always use simple sentences. As we develop our skills we start to use compound and complex sentences. This makes the writing more interesting.

7 Compare these two accounts of the first day at school. Identify:
- the types of sentence used in **A**
- the types of sentence used in **B**.

A I walked through the gates. I was shaking. I was afraid. The school was very big. I looked for my friend. I looked in the playground. I couldn't see her. A teacher came over to me. She smiled at me. She took my hand. She showed me to my classroom. She pointed to where I should sit. Then my friend came in. She sat beside me. I began to feel better.

B As I walked through the gates, I was shaking with fear. The school was very big and, although I looked for my friend in the playground, I couldn't see her. A teacher came over to me and she smiled. Taking my hand, she showed me to my classroom and pointed to where I should sit. Then my friend came in and, as soon as she sat beside me, I began to feel better.

Notice how the writer of **B** has not changed many of the words but has introduced a wider range of sentence structures.

8 a The following paragraph is written in simple sentences. Rewrite it using a range of sentence structures to make it suitable for an older reader.

It was dinner-time. I went into the playground. There were lots of children there. They were all playing. I felt very lonely. My friend had gone home. I had a packed lunch. A boy came over to me. He asked me where I lived. He said his name was John. He asked me my name. I told him. He asked if I had a packed lunch. I nodded. He showed me to the dining room. It was very crowded. He found a table. I began to feel better.

b When you have rewritten the paragraph use different colours to underline:
- simple sentences
- compound sentences
- complex sentences.

3 Sentence sense

Punctuating sentences

When we speak we use our tone of voice and pauses to help our listener follow what we are saying.

When we write we use punctuation to help our reader follow what we have written. We put spaces between words, capital letters at the start of a sentence and full stops at the end. Passage **A** shows what it would be like if we didn't.

We use commas in sentences to mark pauses, and pairs of commas to separate out extra pieces of information. Read passage **B** aloud and notice how commas are used to help the reader to follow the meaning.

A itwasdinnertimeiwentintotheplaygroundtherewerelotsofchildrenthereheywereallplayingifeltverylonelymyfriendhadgonehomeihadapackedlunchaboycameovertomeheaskedmewhereilivedhesaidhisnamewasjohn

B As I walked through the gates, I was shaking with fear. The school was very big and, although I looked for my friend in the playground, I couldn't see her. A teacher came over to me and she smiled. Taking my hand, she showed me to my classroom and pointed to where I should sit. Then my friend came in and, as soon as she sat beside me, I began to feel better.

9 Copy the following sentences and decide where the commas should be placed to help the reader follow the meaning.

> The figures from the company's own nutrition information come amid rising concern about the obesity epidemic that has left two thirds of British adults overweight.
>
> A spokeswoman for Kellogg's which has annual sales of one billion dollars confirmed the differences between the UK and domestic market.
>
> Which? the consumer group said such differences were unacceptable.
>
> In a survey this year Which? found 75 per cent of 270 cereals were high in sugar and a fifth were high in salt.
>
> (The *Independent* 25 October 2006)

Checkpoint

Check your answers to question 9 with a partner. Where you disagree, decide which answer best helps the reader to follow the meaning.

Look back at the paragraph you rewrote in Question 8. Check and correct your use of commas.

Summary

In this unit you have:
- identified simple, compound and complex sentences
- learned how to vary your sentence structures for different readers
- used commas to make the meaning clearer for the reader.

4 Building paragraphs

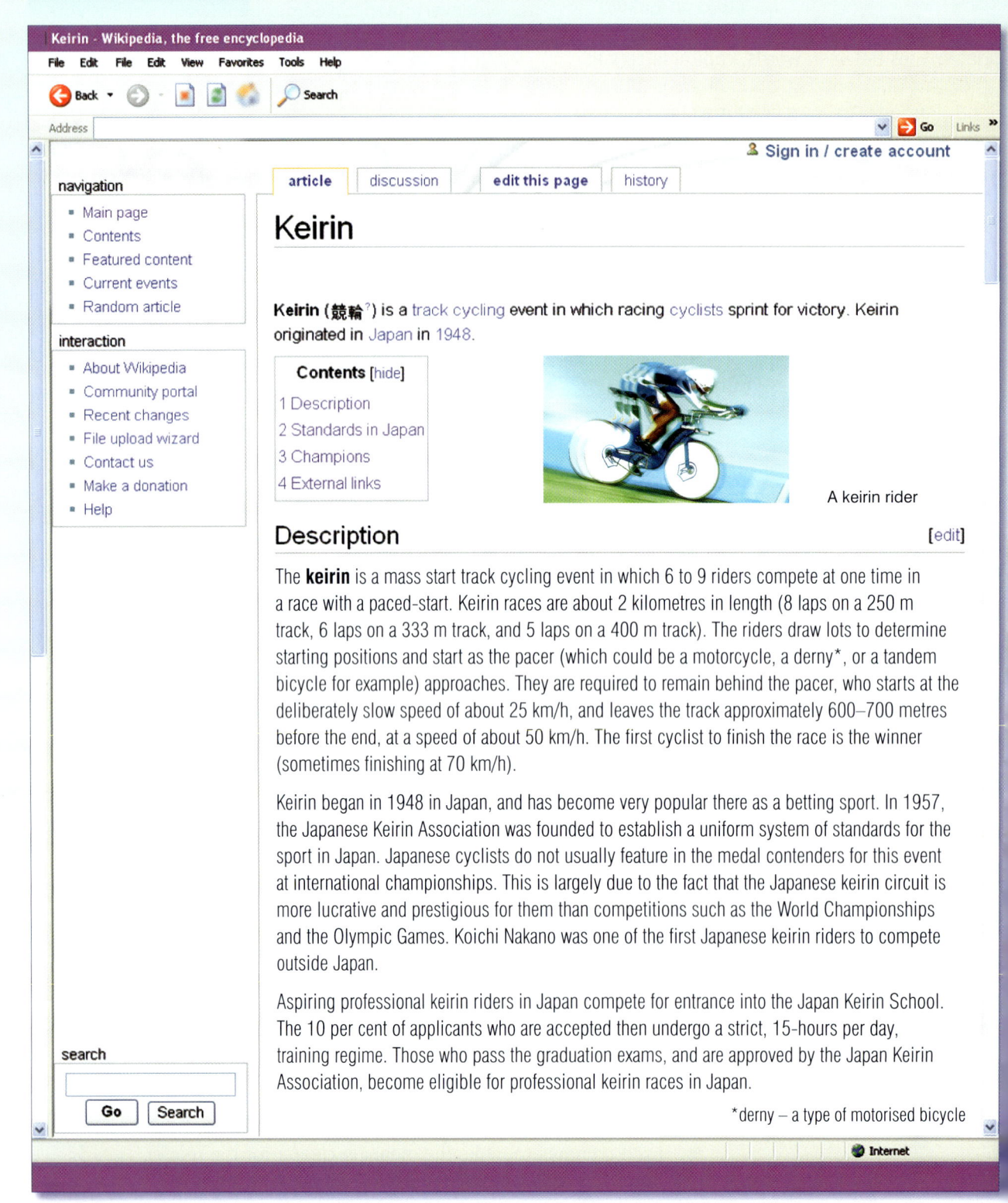

Keirin

Keirin (競輪?) is a track cycling event in which racing cyclists sprint for victory. Keirin originated in Japan in 1948.

Contents [hide]
1 Description
2 Standards in Japan
3 Champions
4 External links

A keirin rider

Description [edit]

The **keirin** is a mass start track cycling event in which 6 to 9 riders compete at one time in a race with a paced-start. Keirin races are about 2 kilometres in length (8 laps on a 250 m track, 6 laps on a 333 m track, and 5 laps on a 400 m track). The riders draw lots to determine starting positions and start as the pacer (which could be a motorcycle, a derny*, or a tandem bicycle for example) approaches. They are required to remain behind the pacer, who starts at the deliberately slow speed of about 25 km/h, and leaves the track approximately 600–700 metres before the end, at a speed of about 50 km/h. The first cyclist to finish the race is the winner (sometimes finishing at 70 km/h).

Keirin began in 1948 in Japan, and has become very popular there as a betting sport. In 1957, the Japanese Keirin Association was founded to establish a uniform system of standards for the sport in Japan. Japanese cyclists do not usually feature in the medal contenders for this event at international championships. This is largely due to the fact that the Japanese keirin circuit is more lucrative and prestigious for them than competitions such as the World Championships and the Olympic Games. Koichi Nakano was one of the first Japanese keirin riders to compete outside Japan.

Aspiring professional keirin riders in Japan compete for entrance into the Japan Keirin School. The 10 per cent of applicants who are accepted then undergo a strict, 15-hours per day, training regime. Those who pass the graduation exams, and are approved by the Japan Keirin Association, become eligible for professional keirin races in Japan.

*derny – a type of motorised bicycle

Keirin extract from *Wikipedia*; http://en.wikipedia.org/

4 Building paragraphs

In this unit ...

You will see how writers use paragraphs to structure their writing and organise their ideas. You will also write your own paragraphs on a subject that interests you.

Read the passage on the opposite page. This is taken from Wikipedia, a free internet-based encyclopaedia. The purpose of the passage is to inform readers about keirin cycling.

Organising sentences into paragraphs

Most writing is organised into paragraphs. This helps the reader to follow more easily the points being made. Each paragraph marks a new stage or idea in the writing. The first sentence of a paragraph is sometimes called the topic sentence. This is because it often gives you a clue as to what the paragraph is going to be about.

1 With a partner, identify and write down what each paragraph in the keirin article is about. Remember to use the topic sentences to help you:

| 1st paragraph | This is about what happens in a keirin race. |

2 Inside a paragraph, sentences should follow each other logically. Here is a sentence breakdown of the first paragraph of the keirin article.

Sentence 1: tells the reader what the keirin is
Sentence 2: gives more information about it
Sentence 3: moves on to the riders in the race and mentions the pacer
Sentence 4: tells you more about the pacer
Sentence 5: tells you about the winning rider.

Do a sentence breakdown like the one above for the second and third paragraphs to find out how the sentences follow each other logically.

3 Highlighting parts of a paragraph can sometimes help you to see the connections between sentences more clearly. For example:

> The **keirin** is a mass start track cycling event in which 6 to 9 riders compete at one time in a race with a paced-start. Keirin races are about 2 kilometres in length (8 laps on a 250 m track, 6 laps on a 333 m track, and 5 laps on a 400 m track). The riders draw lots to determine starting positions and start as the pacer (which could be a motorcycle, a derny*, or a tandem bicycle for example) approaches. They are required to remain behind the pacer, who starts at the deliberately slow speed of about 25 km/h, and leaves the track approximately 600–700 metres before the end, at a speed of about 50 km/h. The first cyclist to finish the race is the winner (sometimes finishing at 70 km/h).

a Look at the words highlighted in pink. These all make a point about the race itself. Now look at the words highlighted in yellow. What are all of these about?

b Find and make lists of all the words that have to do with:
- the pacer
- the speed of the race.

4 Copy the second paragraph and highlight, using different colours, the connections between the sentences. Focus on words that have to do with:
- the keirin
- Japanese cyclists.

English: The Basic Skills

Writing your own paragraphs

You are going to write three paragraphs on a subject of your choice for Wikipedia. Your aim is to inform your reader.

5 a Choose a subject you know something about. It could be any of the following or something completely different:

- A particular type of music or art 
- Computer game(s)
- A football club, dance school or similar
- A particular type of job or career
- An environmental issue 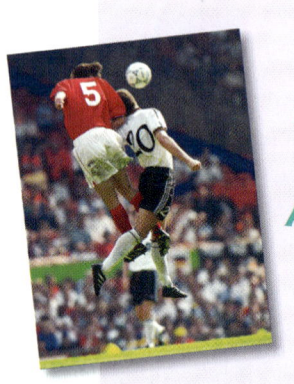
- A town, city or country 
- UFOs
- A sport
- MSN
- Fashion

b In order to inform your reader you need to tell them things about your chosen subject. Make a list of the different things you know about it.

6 Examine your list.
a You need to choose three main areas under which you can group your ideas. Here are a few examples to help you:

Subject	Group 1	Group 2	Group 3
Football club	History of the club	About the players	About the fans
A job/career	What the job/career involves	Qualifications needed	The advantages/disadvantages of this job/career
A city	Geographical details	Places to visit/attractions	Transport

b Draw up your own grid like the one above. Put in your subject and three groups of ideas. These will be your three paragraphs.

7 Make a note of:
- how you are going to start each paragraph
- the order in which you are going to give the details to your reader.

Remember, your order should be logical and you need to give enough detail to inform your reader well. Aim to write four to six sentences in each paragraph.

20

4 Building paragraphs

8 a Write the first draft of your three paragraphs. A new paragraph can be shown in two ways.

1 You can indent the first word so that it starts a little way in from the margin, for example:

> *Paris is the capital city of France. It is situated on the banks of the River Seine in the north of France.*

This is the form normally used in handwritten work.

2 You can leave a line space between two paragraphs. This form is sometimes used in word-processed work, as can be seen in the passage on page 18.

b Reread each paragraph after writing it. Check you have given your information in a clear and logical order.

9 In the passage on page 18 the word 'derny' is explained by the use of a footnote. Use footnotes to explain any words your reader might not know.

Group activity

10 a Once you have finished, ask two or three people to read your writing.

b Use the following questions and answers to record their comments:

Writing score card

Did it inform?	Very well/Fairly well/Not very well
Was the information expressed clearly?	Very clear/Quite clear/Not very clear
Did it follow a logical order?	All the time/Most of the time/Some of the time
Was enough detail given?	Yes/No
Was it organised into three clear paragraphs?	Yes/No
Were unfamiliar words explained?	Yes/No

11 Use the comments readers have made on your paragraphs to help you write your final draft.

Summary

In this unit you have:
- seen how paragraphs can be used to organise writing
- seen how sentences are organised within paragraphs
- used paragraphs to structure your own writing.

5 Planning control

In this unit ...
you will learn how to plan, organise and draft writing in a series of careful steps.

The ability to plan is an important life skill. You may need to plan a journey or a holiday or how to progress in your career. The ability to plan is also an important factor in successful writing. You need to plan to ensure your writing does exactly what it is intended to do. Your plan is for your use, so you need to develop the form of planning that suits you best. Below you can see three different plans made by students in response to the same task.

Task: write an article for a magazine aimed at teenagers in which you argue that students should be taught to drive at school or college

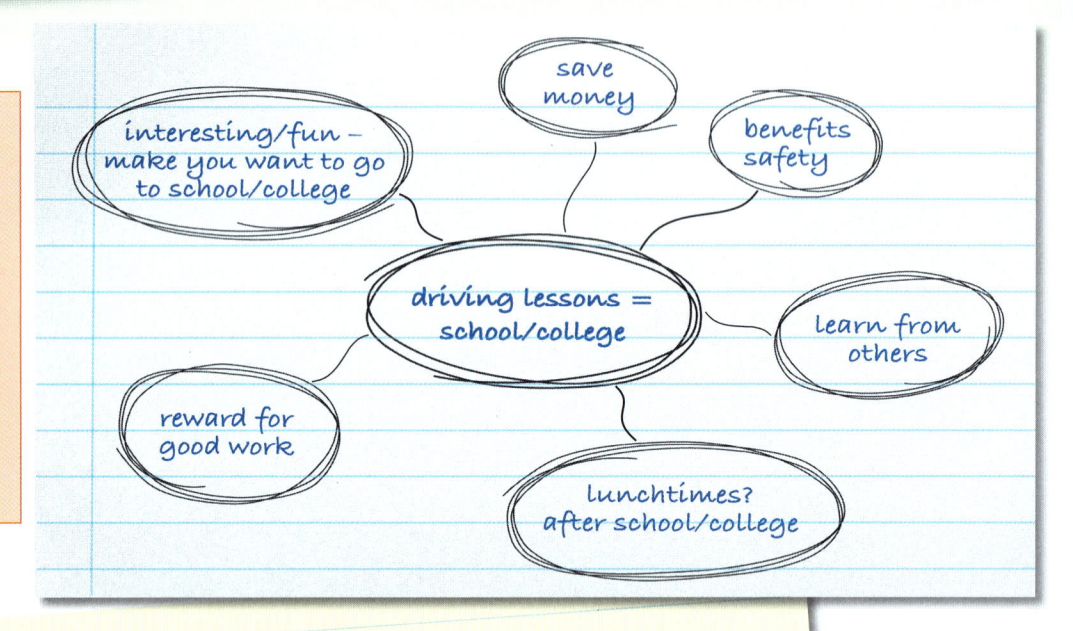

Spider diagram centred on "driving lessons = school/college" with branches:
- save money
- benefits safety
- interesting/fun – make you want to go to school/college
- learn from others
- reward for good work
- lunchtimes? after school/college

Purpose: argue – students taught to drive at school

Audience: teenagers

Form: magazine article

Make a change from ord. lessons – people wld want to go – teachers might not like it – costs? Where wld you drive – no space – safer for students – cld learn about cars & how to look after them. **Bored with life studying – then here's your chance**

---

1. Make it lively for teenagers – some informal language
2. Argue using key points – fun – safe – cheaper
3. Make up e.g.s – someone who did and someone who didn't
4. Think about counterarguments – where? when?
5. Involve reader – use you & rhetorical qus

5 Planning control

Identifying purpose, audience and form

The first step in planning writing is to identify the intended purpose, audience and form of your writing.

The **purpose** is the reason or reasons you have for writing the text.

The **audience** is the intended reader or readers for whom you are writing.

The **form** is the kind of text you are being asked to write.

1 a Now read the following tasks. For each one identify the:
- purpose
- audience
- form.

Task 1
Write a letter to a teachers' magazine in which you inform teachers about what life is really like for people of your age.

Task 2
Write an article for a school or college website in which you argue that the music you like is the best there is.

Task 3
Write a letter to the governors of your school or college persuading them to upgrade the facilities for students.

b Check your answers with a partner before moving on.

Gathering ideas

The next step is to gather ideas connected to the task. This is the thinking stage where you get as many helpful ideas together as you can. You do not need to use them all in your writing, but you can draw on them and you won't get stuck for ideas halfway through.

Here are the ideas one student, Craig, came up with in response to Task 1, above.

- going out — where? girls — late nights
- school work — coursework — pressure — nagging
- football — Dad — mates — good times
- 'What life is really like'
- family — Nan ill — Mum upset — helping out (sometimes)
- what adults say — untrue — don't understand
- pressures — clothes — drinking — work — girls again!

2 a Choose either Task 2 or 3 from question **1a** above. Jot down as many different ideas as you can think of in relation to your chosen title. You could use one of the sample plan forms on page 22.

b Share your ideas with another student. Ask them for any further suggestions to add to your notes.

English: The Basic Skills

Organising your ideas

The next stage is to decide which ideas you are going to use and the order in which you are going to write them.

Here is how Craig organised his ideas:

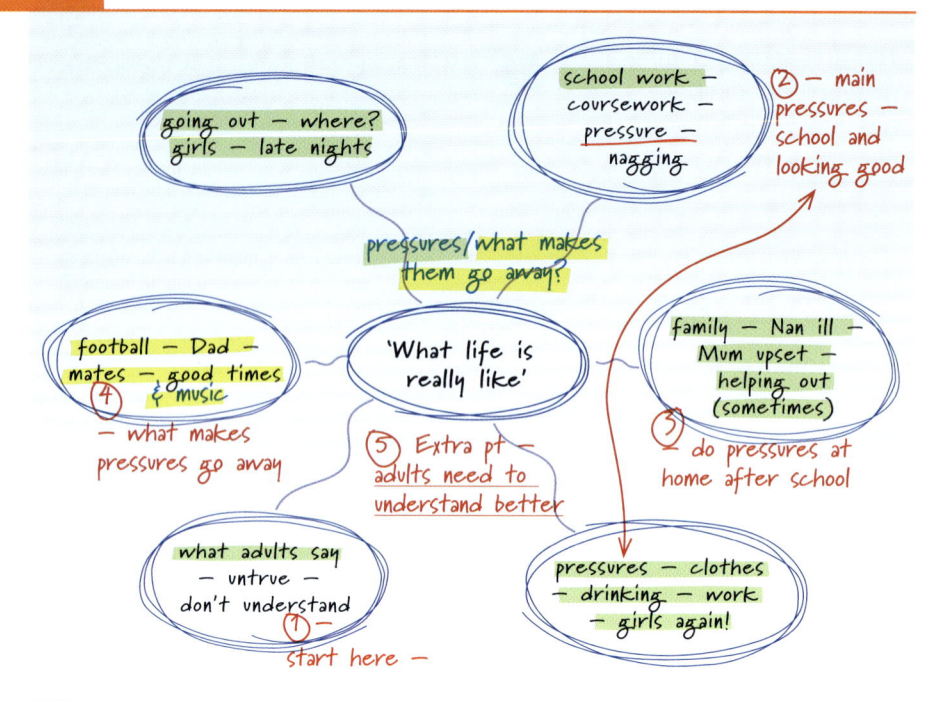

- going out — where? girls — late nights
- school work — coursework — pressure — nagging
- ② — main pressures — school and looking good
- pressures/what makes them go away?
- football — Dad — mates — good times & music ④ — what makes pressures go away
- 'What life is really like'
- family — Nan ill — Mum upset — helping out (sometimes) ③ — do pressures at home after school
- ⑤ Extra pt — adults need to understand better
- what adults say — untrue — don't understand ① — start here —
- pressures — clothes — drinking — work — girls again!

3 Now look at your own ideas from question 2.
   a Cross out any you no longer want to include.
   b Group the others in the best order for writing.
   c Decide if there is anything else you could add to improve your writing.

4 Paragraphs are essential in writing and you need to plan for them.
   a Read the paragraph plan that Craig made next.

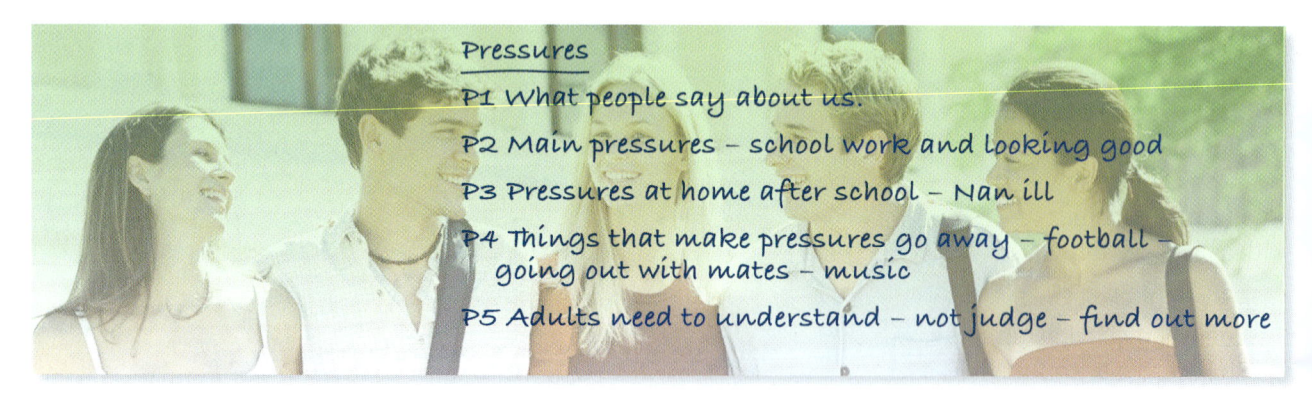

> Pressures
> P1 What people say about us.
> P2 Main pressures — school work and looking good
> P3 Pressures at home after school — Nan ill
> P4 Things that make pressures go away — football — going out with mates — music
> P5 Adults need to understand — not judge — find out more

   b Now make your own paragraph plan. Plan for about five clear and coherent paragraphs.

Drafting

There are three main stages in writing: the first draft, redrafting, the final draft. The process of drafting is easier if you use a PC.

5 You are going to write for the task you chose on page 23. Work through the three stages on page 25. Follow Stage 1 to write your first draft. Follow Stage 2 to redraft your writing and Stage 3 to produce your final draft.

5 Planning control

Stage 1: the first draft
Using your paragraph plan as your guide, write a first draft of your piece. Your aim here is to put your ideas into sentences and to make sure that your writing is appropriate to your purpose, audience and form. After each paragraph, read to check for clear sense.

Stage 2: redrafting
Exchange your writing with two or three other students. Ask them to list two things you do well and two things you could do to improve it.

Here's an example of how Craig redrafted his first paragraph after others had read it:

> ~~People~~ **Teachers** are always ~~going on~~ **complaining** about teenagers, saying that they are lazy and don't do the things they should ~~do~~ **be doing**. I don't think ~~it's~~ **this is** fair. ~~and~~ I think it's time ~~people~~ **teachers** stopped and thought about what teenagers' lives are really like. **Do they ever take the time to find out?** Perhaps if they did find out they wouldn't ~~say the kinds of things they say~~ **be so quick to criticise us**.

Now make improvements to your writing, taking into account the comments your readers made. Here are some extra questions to consider.
- Have you used the form stated in the task?
- Is your writing targeted at your audience?
- Is your writing focused on your purpose?
- How can you make it more interesting?
- Should some points be developed further?
- Can you make your opening and closing more effective?

Cross out things you no longer want to keep and add in extras.

Stage 3: the final draft
When you have made the changes for improvement, write the final draft.
- Take care with handwriting, spelling and punctuation.
- Re-read each paragraph after writing to check for clear communication and accuracy.

Checkpoint
Ask a partner to read your final draft and to let you know if there are any errors you had not noticed. Correct these.

Summary

In this unit you have:
- thought about the importance of planning
- planned your own writing
- redrafted a first draft, making improvements
- written and checked a final draft.

25

6 Correcting correctly

In this unit ...
you are going to examine some of the most frequently made errors in writing. You will correct them and check your corrections are right to ensure that your writing is accurate.

Very few writers get it right first time all the time. They make mistakes and have to revise their writing for accuracy of grammar, spelling and punctuation. The trick is to:

- develop your skills in spotting your mistakes
- be aware of your weak areas – the things you often get wrong
- develop your skills in correcting correctly!

Verb-tense agreement

A **verb** is a part of a sentence. We use verbs to:

- express an action, for example:

    He **kicks** the ball.

- express feelings and states of mind, for example:

    She **loves** her mum.

A **tense** is a verb form that indicates time. For example:

he **walked** (past)

he **walks** (present)

he **will walk** (future)

To make clear sense in your writing, the verb form must be in the correct tense.

She makes a cake last week. ✗
She made a cake last week. ✓

1 Correct the following sentences so that the highlighted verb is in the correct tense.
  a He walked down the path and **looks** through the window.
  b When the sun goes down the desert **came** to life.
  c The couple **see** the film last week.
  d The teacher told them to close their eyes and **listened**.
  e She **realised** there are two unused discs in the pack.
  f When the shop was opened, the crowds **push** forward.

Subject-verb agreement

The **subject** in a sentence is the person or thing about which something is said.

The **verb** should always agree with the subject.

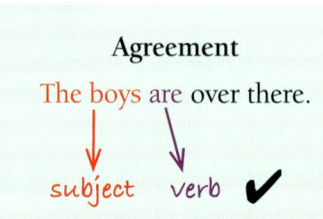

Agreement	Non-agreement
The boys are over there.	The boys is over there.
subject verb ✓	subject verb ✗

6 Correcting correctly

2 Correct the following sentences so that the verb agrees with the subject.
   a Both the teacher and the student was in the canteen at the time.
   b Someone have taken the pens away.
   c Art classes is very interesting.
   d The boys kicks the ball against the wall.
   e John and Elaine has been to the shop.
   f The dog were waiting by the front door.

Checkpoint

Check your answers with a partner. If you have different answers, decide who is right and make the necessary corrections.

Using what you have learned about verb-tense and subject-verb agreement, work on your own to copy and complete these sentences.

A tense is …

To make clear sense in your writing, the verb form must be in …

The subject in a sentence is …

The verb should always agree with …

Correct your spelling

Many people believe they have a problem with spelling. The truth is that most people can learn how to spell words correctly by following rules or using simple strategies for remembering or checking.

Spelling mistakes are often made for very simple reasons. For example:

a letter may be left out: crossing ✔   crosing ✘

a letter may be added: business ✔   bussiness ✘

a letter or letters that make the same sound may be used instead of the correct letter: grown ✔   groan ✘

3 Try this simple test. In the following piece of writing there are twelve spelling mistakes – far more than most people usually make. The misspelt words are highlighted. Write them down. Underline the mistake and write the correct spelling beside each word.

For example: armys   armies

London: Having invaded Britain almost 2,000 years ago, the Roman armys then built a town to make the crosing over the River Thames safe. This town was calld Londinium, the city we now know as London. Bye 1100, the city of London had groan in size to become the capital of the hole country. London is now an importent bussiness centre and its influence in polatics, culture, educacion, fashion and entetainment helps to make it one of the key global citys.

English: The Basic Skills

Spelling rules

Occasionally, spelling mistakes are made because the writer does not know the rules.

The writer of the London passage has misspelt armies (armys ✗) and cities (citys ✗). They don't know the rules regarding plurals of words ending in y.

If a word ending in y has a consonant before the last letter, change the y to an i and add es.

If a word ending in y has a vowel before the last letter, just add s.

4 Using the above rules, write the plurals of the following words:

day   donkey   try   toy   tray
party   anxiety   essay   baby
bully   body   casualty   country
play   factory   reality   photocopy
monkey   conspiracy   memory

Checkpoint

Check your answers to activities 3 and 4 with a partner. If your answers are different, decide who is correct and make the necessary corrections.

Common mistakes

People often make the same mistakes many times. If they can learn the rules and remember their mistakes, they can spell the words correctly in future.

5 The following student spells many words correctly. However, he also makes the same mistakes many times. Read his piece of writing and identify the mistakes. What two tips would you give this student to help improve his spelling?

> The first time the theif broke into the house he dident beleive what he saw. For a breif moment he thought he was dreaming. Now he was back and this time he couldent fail. He hadent made a sound as he'd climbed the stairs and it was with a huge sigh of releif that he silently opened the door.

Checkpoint

It is important to know how well you spell and where you are most likely to make mistakes. Look back over the writing you have done recently. Make a list of any spelling mistakes you have made and the corrections. Can you identify any patterns? Remember to keep a close eye on these types of word when checking your spelling in the future.

6 Correcting correctly

Accurate sentence punctuation

Punctuation makes it easier for a reader to follow the writing. The first step in checking for accurate punctuation is to make sure that capital letters, full stops and question marks are correctly placed.

6 Rewrite the following reply to a wedding invitation. Put in capital letters, full stops and question marks where needed.

> dear kate and ian
> many thanks for the invitation to your wedding on june 13th unfortunately, john and i will be away on holiday in greece that weekend we get back on the 20th and would love to see you sometime after that when do you get back from your honeymoon would saturday 27th suit you let me know and we can sort something out have a fantastic day,
> chloe and john

Checkpoint

Check your corrections with a partner. Where they are different, decide who is correct and make any necessary changes.

Summary

In this unit you have:
- corrected mistakes in verb-tense and subject-verb agreement
- identified and corrected spelling mistakes
- identified and corrected punctuation mistakes.

7 Story time

In this unit …
you will read a narrative text in detail and identify the main points and ideas in it. You will identify the order in which the story is narrated and consider features of language use. You will also summarise and retell the story.

Read the article below carefully. It is an example of a narrative text.

I feel a right Charlie

How it took six firemen to free the toddler with his head stuck in a cone

by **Luke Salkeld**

TO Charlie Thomas, it must have seemed a wizard idea.

Spotting a discarded traffic cone, the imaginative three-year-old immediately saw its potential as an impromptu Harry Potter outfit.

But after placing it carefully on his head to show his family, the magic soon disappeared.

The plastic cone became firmly stuck and despite the best efforts of the toddler's parents, it refused to budge.

Perhaps a Potter-style cry of 'Expelliarmus!' might have helped.

But in the end they had to call the fire brigade – and it took a crew of six half an hour to release Charlie using cutting tools and pliers.

Yesterday, his mother said Charlie was left with a slight bruising to his head – and pride – after his attempt to mimic his Hogwarts hero.

Louisa Thomas, 34, said: "He loves Harry Potter and when he put the cone on he was so pleased with himself, it was very sweet. But when we couldn't get it off it was a bit scary.

The bank worker added: 'He was very good while the firemen were there and he didn't panic. They got him out by pouring water down the top of the cone for lubrication and cutting the rim.

Charlie, who turned three at the weekend, was on a family outing to fly his brand new kite when the incident happened.

After lunch with his parents, grandparents and sisters Emily, eight, and Isabella, four, the family visited a playing field near their home in Cullompton, Devon. But before the kite was in the air, he had picked up the cone from the side of the field and put it on his head.

Mrs Thomas and her husband Martin, a car sprayer, tried wiggling him free, pulling the cone and using soapy water.

When they thought their only option was to cut the cone, they called the fire brigade for help.

Mr Thomas said Charlie was very excited by Halloween which, combined with his love for Harry Potter, meant the cone was an irresistible temptation.

He said, "My first reaction was laughter. It wasn't until I got over to him and realised it was really stuck that I got worried."

Conehead: Charlie Thomas in a photo taken by his mother as he waits for the fire brigade

© Daily Mail, *October 23 2007, by Luke Salkeld*

7 Story time

Understanding the story

Narrative texts often include many points of detail to make the story interesting and entertaining.

To make sure you have understood the detail of the story correctly, answer the following multiple-choice questions. Each question gives you four possible answers but only one of these is correct.

1 Charlie put the cone on his head because:
  a he wanted to shout "Expelliarmus"
  b he didn't want to fly his kite
  c he wanted to be like Harry Potter
  d he wanted to celebrate Halloween.

2 Charlie visited the playing field with at least:
  a one relative   b two relatives
  c four relatives   d six relatives.

3 Charlie was released from the cone by:
  a wiggling him free
  b pouring water down the top of the cone and cutting the rim
  c calling the fire brigade
  d using soapy water.

4 Martin Thomas's first reaction was:
  a worry   b anger   c fear   d laughter.

5 Mr and Mrs Thomas called the fire brigade when:
  a they stopped laughing
  b they'd run out of soapy water
  c they thought they would have to cut the cone
  d Charlie complained of bruising.

6 The fire crew took:
  a six hours to free Charlie   b six minutes to free Charlie
  c half an hour to free Charlie   d three hours to free Charlie.

7 The main purpose of this text is to:
  a tell the reader an interesting story
  b warn children about the dangers of wearing a cone
  c advertise Harry Potter
  d praise the fire brigade.

English: The Basic Skills

The order of events

Chronological order means the sequence in which events happened. Stories are sometimes told in chronological order.

When the sequence of events is not given in the order in which they happened, the story is **non-chronological**.

The story about Charlie is told in non-chronological order.

8 Below are eight events taken from the story in the order in which they appear. Copy and complete the following table by sorting the extracts into chronological order. The first one is done for you.

a Spotting a discarded traffic cone, the imaginative three-year-old immediately saw its potential as an impromptu Harry Potter outfit.

b But after placing it carefully on his head to show his family, the magic soon disappeared.

c The plastic cone became firmly stuck and despite the best efforts of the toddler's parents, it refused to budge.

d It took a crew of six half an hour to release Charlie using cutting tools and pliers.

e Charlie, who turned three at the weekend, was on a family outing to fly his brand new kite when the incident happened.

f After lunch with his parents, grandparents and sisters Emily, eight, and Isabella, four, the family visited a playing field near their home in Cullompton, Devon.

g Mrs Thomas and her husband Martin, a car sprayer, tried wiggling him free, pulling the cone and using soapy water.

h When they thought their only option was to cut the cone, they called the fire brigade for help.

a	b	c	d	e	f	g	h
				1			

Using adjectives for description

When telling the story of Charlie and the traffic cone, the writer uses a range of adjectives to help the reader picture the situation, for example:

Spotting a discarded traffic cone, the imaginative three-year-old immediately saw its potential as an impromptu Harry Potter outfit.

9 Identify and write down the adjectives in the following sentences from the article below:

The plastic cone became firmly stuck and despite the best efforts of the toddler's parents, it refused to budge.

Charlie, who turned three at the weekend, was on a family outing to fly his brand new kite when the incident happened.

Mr Thomas said Charlie was very excited about Halloween which, combined with his love for Harry Potter, meant the cone was an irresistible temptation.

7 Story time

> **Checkpoint**
>
> Check your answers to questions 1 to 9 with another student. If your answers differ, look back and decide which answers are correct.

Summarising ideas

When writing for a newspaper, journalists have to fill a certain amount of space. This directly influences how much detail they give the reader. This story might also be told on the radio but would probably only get a short period of airtime.

10 Your task is to write the script, based on the story of Charlie and the cone, for a radio presenter to read. The story, when read aloud, should last no longer than 40 seconds. Follow these steps:
- Identify the main points of the story that would need to be included if the listener is to understand what happened. Make a note of these.
- To make the story shorter and more focused, tell it in chronological order. Your answers to question 8 will help you do this.
- Write the script. Remember to use standard English.
- Practise reading your story. It's a light-hearted story and you might want to read it in a way that reflects this. Remember you only have 40 seconds of airtime so you may need to edit the story.

> **Checkpoint**
>
> With two or three other students, take it in turns to read your story as though you were a radio presenter. Decide between you whose story was most suitable for a radio broadcast. Give three reasons for your choice.

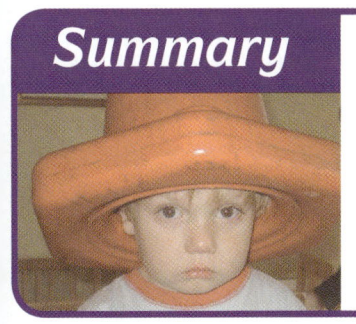

Summary

In this unit you have:
- read and understood the main points and details of a story
- identified the chronological order of events
- identified the use of adjectives to describe
- summarised the story and presented it appropriately for a different medium.

8 Taking a break

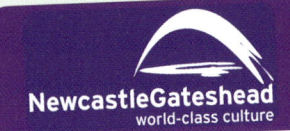

NewcastleGateshead
world-class culture

Welcome to NewcastleGateshead
One of *Time Magazine*'s Secret Capitals of Europe…

Located in North East England, Newcastle (on the north bank of the River Tyne) and Gateshead (on the south bank) have been transformed into a single visitor destination called NewcastleGateshead.

NewcastleGateshead is a mix of the modern and historic, renowned for its excellent shopping and amazing nightlife. But NewcastleGateshead has much more to offer – explore the beautiful architecture including the ancient city walls and castle; enjoy the stunning quayside with its waterfront bars and galleries; and don't miss the fantastic public art such as the Angel of the North. With a year-long programme of festivals and events there is always something going on.

Keswick

Near museums and shops, this recently refurbished accommodation is ideal for exploring Borrowdale and Derwentwater

Great for:
Fantastic scenery, vibrant town, theatre, great family location in North Lakes

Prices from:
Adult: £16.50
Under 18: £12.50
Price includes breakfast

yha

Description:
Combine extensive walking with a wealth of evening entertainment at this location, which sits on the banks of the River Greta. There's plenty of walking here in the northern Lakes – if you need tempting then Skiddaw, one of the highest mountains in the Lake District, forms an impressive backdrop to the view from the property. It's just a few minutes' walk into the town centre, where you'll find plenty of pubs, a cinema and a theatre.

Ragdale Hall Health Hydro

8 **Taking a break**

Two-night weekend spa break at Ragdale Hall – winner of 'Health Spa of the Year' – voucher

Take a luxury two-night weekend spa break at Ragdale Hall and enjoy a choice of treatment, breakfast, lunch, dinner and unlimited use of all the fabulous facilities.

Situated in the beautiful Leicestershire countryside, **Ragdale Hall Health Hydro** is totally unique. Combining state-of-the-art facilities with the charm of traditional Victorian architecture, Ragdale Hall is one of the most luxurious and relaxing health spas in the country, the ultimate destination for luxury spa breaks.

Prices from £299 to £419

Benidorm holidays

Benidorm prices start from £99 for seven nights!

Benidorm, located on the Costa Blanca on the east coast of Spain, is the largest and liveliest resort in the area, attracting a million British visitors every year. Although tourism has taken away a lot of the resort's Spanish identity, Benidorm still offers everything that tourists require on a package holiday and is blessed with fantastic sandy beaches, an amazing array of entertainment and a wealth of accommodation choices. Benidorm continues to be a favourite with all types of holidaymakers, from the young 18–30 crowd lured by the prospect of the pulsating all-night clubs and discos, to the pensioners who come to enjoy the wonderful climate during the winter months and families who appreciate the great beaches and convenient facilities.

OUTDOOR ADVENTURE

Multi-Activity and Surf Centre, Widemouth Bay, Bude, Cornwall. Self-catering

The Centre's setting is incredible. On arrival you will immediately find yourself surrounded by a magnificent, naturally wild, coastal environment. Our cliff-top centre overlooks the Atlantic Ocean and the 10 acres of beautiful Centre grounds have been designated a Site of Special Scientific Interest by English Nature and a European area of conservation.

Look out across the Atlantic Ocean and feel alive!

Atlantic Court
A unique self-catering opportunity
Rent Atlantic Court for a winter break
Get a group of friends or families together and enjoy our spectacular setting in Cornwall out of the holiday season - maybe celebrate an occasion on our cliff top!
From £4.21 per person per night!!

English: The Basic Skills

In this unit ...

you will read and consider a range of options for a short break holiday. You will discuss these options in a group and arrive at a final decision about which break the group should take.

Many people take holidays with friends. There is a huge range of types of holiday and destination. A range of possible holiday places is printed on pages 34–35. Read these carefully. You will be choosing your holiday from them.

Preparing for group discussion

Before you get together with your group you need to do some independent thinking and preparation. Consider questions 1 to 3 to prepare for working with your group.

1 a Consider the advantages and disadvantages of each holiday destination advertised on pages 34 to 35. Make a table like the one below and make a note of your ideas.

DESTINATION	ADVANTAGES	DISADVANTAGES
NewcastleGateshead		
Keswick YHA		

b Using your table to help you, decide and list the order of your preference for these holidays. List the reasons that helped you to decide your first choice.

2 It's not always easy to work as part of a group. Here are some of the qualities that help to ensure a group works effectively. Think about how well you perform in groups and where your weaknesses are. List the three qualities you are going to try to focus on developing in your group discussion.

Listen carefully.   *Express ideas clearly.*   *Allow others to express their views.*
Give everyone the opportunity to speak.   *Help move the discussion forward to reach decisions.*
Be prepared to compromise.   *Respond appropriately to what others say.*
Use language effectively to argue your case and persuade others.

Taking part in a group discussion

You have thought about some of the qualities needed for successful group discussion and have chosen three areas to develop. Think about how you are going to develop those areas and then move on to the group activity.

3 You are going to work in a group of three or four. Your task is to come to an agreement through discussion and negotiation. You will have thirty minutes in which to agree which holiday you would choose. Read the 'Do' and 'Don't' lists on page 37 and follow steps A–F.

8 Taking a break

Group activity

DO

Show you've listened, for example by saying, *'I understand what you meant when you said that ... but I think that ...'.*

Clarify anything you're not sure about, for example by saying, *'When you said ..., did you mean ...?'*

Try to persuade by introducing new ideas, for example by saying, *'Have you thought about ...?'*

Try to persuade by getting others to picture the holiday you have in mind, for example by saying, *'Just imagine how good it would be to ...'.*

Include others in the group by using the first person plural 'we', for example by saying, *'If we went there we could ...'.*

Encourage quieter members of the group to join in and contribute.

DON'T

Try to force your ideas on others by doing all the talking.

Shout or be impolite.

Sulk and stop talking if things are not going your way.

Sit and say nothing or offer very little.

A Form a group of three or four. To help you complete the task in time, appoint one person to let the group know when:
- fifteen minutes have passed
- five minutes are left.

B Take it in turns to say which of the holidays you would like to go on and the reasons for your choice. Also make clear which holiday you would least like to go on and why. Keep your own notes on what each person says – you may need to try and persuade some individuals to change their minds later and you may want to refer to the reasons for their choices.

C Once each person has stated their preference, the discussion is open to the group. You all need to be prepared to discuss, negotiate and compromise if you are to agree on a holiday. You may have to abandon your first preference, particularly if others say they simply cannot afford it. Use the lists on the left to help you get the most from your discussion.

D Once you get the fifteen-minute warning, you need to start making decisions. If you want, you can appoint one person to draw the ideas of the group together and make notes. You now have five minutes to place the holidays in an agreed order with the most popular choice first and the least popular choice last.

E Take it in turns to say when you would most like to go on the holiday. Compromise is essential here. A sister's wedding is a more important factor than missing a favourite TV programme! When you get the five-minute warning, you need to come to your final decision. If you want, you can get one person to draw the ideas of the group together.

F By the end of the thirty minutes you should have agreed where you are going and when you are going.

Checkpoint

Look back at the three qualities of group discussion that you chose in activity 2. Write a short report assessing how well you did in each of the three areas in the Group activity. When you have finished writing your report, swap it with another member of your group. Ask them if they agree with your assessment (✔) or not (✗). If they don't agree with your assessment, ask them to explain why.

Summary

In this unit you have:
- considered a range of options for a short break holiday
- prioritised your personal choices
- given your point of view and listened to that of others
- responded to the points of view of others
- arrived at a decision through negotiation and compromise.

9 Finding information

Itineraries

Manhattan is easy to explore if you're going uptown or downtown – it's when you want to go crosstown that things get complicated! Most New Yorkers get by with a combination of subway, bus and foot transport (with the occasional cab thrown in) and your best bet is to do the same. The city is bursting with fabulous things to see and do, but don't forget that strolling is a big part of life in NYC – factor in time to saunter the streets.

Pick up a MetroCard (p114) from any newsstand or subway station and start planning; an efficient way to sightsee is to take a bus or subway train to an area you want to explore and then hoof it from sight to sight. When you're ready for a change, go to a totally different part of town and soak it up.

When I grow up, I want to be a statue

First Time
Head to Lower Manhattan to check out the Statue of Liberty and Ellis Island (or jump on the Staten Island Ferry for a quick drive-by look if lines are too long for the full tour). Have a bite at South St Seaport and inhale the briny atmosphere while waiting for the M15 bus to Chinatown. From there explore Tribeca, Soho and Little Italy. As dusk approaches get to the Empire State Building for sunset and then hit Times Sq for a neon-lit dinner (and maybe a show).

Uptown
Greet the morning from Riverside Park, then check out Cathedral of St John the Divine in Morningside Heights. From there, it's two steps to Harlem and a history lesson at Schomberg Center. Soul food awaits at Sylvia's, and don't forget the Apollo Theater, Striver's Row and the Studio Museum. A cup of java at Settepani's, and then hit the Museum Mile on the Upper East Side. Finish with a before-dinner stroll along Central Park.

Downtown
Breakfast in the West Village and then window-shop to Washington Sq Park. Move on to the East Village, following St Marks Pl into Tompkins Sq. Cross Houston St for a late lunch at Schiller's, gallery hopping on Rivington, drinks in Nolita, and then catch a cab to the Meatpacking District for some nightclubbing. Stave off midnight munchies at Florent.

Worst of New York City
NYC does have a few things that can work your nerves:
- MetroCards that won't swipe: happens all the time, but don't even think about jumping that turnstile – somebody *is* watching.
- Subway delays: that local train that suddenly became an express? Now it's out of service.
- Sidewalk smoking: it's everywhere, particularly at night when barflies light up outside.

Highlights

STATUE OF LIBERTY (4, A3)
Presented to the USA in 1886 as a gift from France, the Statue of Liberty, engraved with the words of Emma Lazarus ('Give me your tired, your poor, Your huddled masses yearning to breathe free'), has welcomed millions of immigrants to their new home and still inspires awe in all who behold it. *Liberty Enlightening the World* is the statue's official name, and it was sculpted by Frederic-Auguste Bartholdi (Gustav Eiffel designed the iron skeleton). It stands 305ft (93m) tall and weighs 225 tons. To just stroll around the statue you only need ferry tickets; to go inside you must make a 'Time Pass' reservation with the National Parks Service. The 'Time Pass' is good for one hour (you stipulate the hour you want, say 9am to 10am, and as long as you arrive at the statue before 10am, you'll be allowed in), offering two guided tour options (both are free). One tour goes through the promenade, into the statue's pedestal and then out to surrounding Fort Wood. The other tour includes a stop at the **Observatory Deck**, which is 24 steps above the museum and features entrancing views – almost as good as those from the crown (which is no longer open to the public).

The **museum** has great exhibits detailing Lady Liberty's history and the grounds, while small, are verdant and inviting on a sunny day. The ferries loop between this island, Ellis Island and Manhattan with spectacular views all the way. For the best photos, sit on the right going out and the left coming back. Be aware: lines for the ferry can be very long and security checks add more delays, so head out early and be prepared to wait. For good views without delays, take the Staten Island Ferry (free) or grab a New York Water Taxi (p114) for a drive-by experience.

DON'T MISS
Castle Clinton National Monument, built as a fort in 1807 in Battery Park, is a visitor center and ticket booth for ferries to Ellis Island and the Statue of Liberty. Look for **The Immigrants** near the entrance, a renowned sculpture by Luis Sanguino depicting strangers huddled together and drawing solace from each other as they wait hopefully for admittance to America.

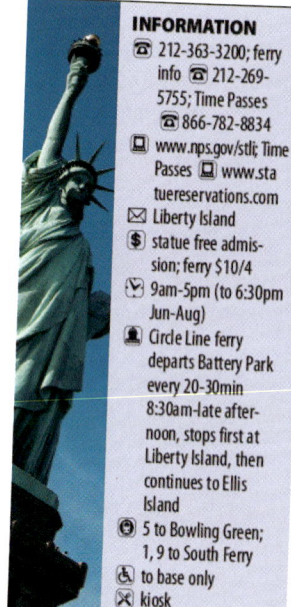

INFORMATION
- ☎ 212-363-3200; ferry info ☎ 212-269-5755; Time Passes ☎ 866-782-8834
- www.nps.gov/stli; Time Passes www.statuereservations.com
- Liberty Island
- $ statue free admission; ferry $10/4
- 9am-5pm (to 6:30pm Jun-Aug)
- Circle Line ferry departs Battery Park every 20-30min 8:30am-late afternoon, stops first at Liberty Island, then continues to Ellis Island
- 5 to Bowling Green; 1, 9 to South Ferry
- to base only
- kiosk

9 Finding information

In this unit ...
you will use different techniques to find information and identify how the main points are organised in different texts.

The way we read something depends on our reason for reading it. Sometimes we read a text to find out a particular piece of information. When we do this, we don't read every word closely. We might focus on key words, or sub-headings, or alphabetical order to help us find what we need.

Scanning a text

If we are looking for a particular piece of information, our eyes move quickly over the whole text until they focus on the key words that locate the detail we are looking for. This type of reading is called scanning.

1 Scan the travel writing text on the opposite page to find the answers to these questions as quickly as you can. The key words you are looking for are printed in bold in the questions.
   a Where can you pick up a **MetroCard**?
   b What is the **official name** of the **Statue of Liberty**?
   c Where would you find the **Cathedral of St John the Divine**?
   d What was built as a fort in **1807**?
   e How long does the **'Time Pass'** last for?

2 Now find the answers to the following five questions. This time, you will need to identify the key words yourself.
   a Where is the Circle Line ferry's first stop?
   b What would you do at the Meatpacking District?
   c What number bus could you catch from South St Seaport to Chinatown?
   d What is the name of the sculpture made by Luis Sanguino?
   e How tall is the Statue of Liberty?

Using sub-headings

In order to scan texts quickly we need to know how the information is organised. The information in the travel writing text is organised using sub-headings. Sub-headings help the reader to find the information he or she is looking for quickly.

3 a What four sub-headings are used for 'Itineraries'?
   b How do the sub-headings help the reader?
   c Think of two reasons which would explain why some of the material is organised by sub-headings and shaded boxes.

4 Imagine you are writing an account about your life and want to organise the information under sub-headings. Below are two examples of sub-headings you could use. Think of five more:

> My birth
> Primary School

English: The Basic Skills

Improving your sub-headings

Sub-headings can be made more interesting through the use of alliteration, exaggeration, rhyme, rhetorical questions and humour. On the right are just a few examples:

Sub-heading	Alternatives
My birth	In trouble from the start
	And then there were three!
Primary School	Tears, fears and cheers
	Friends forever

5 Make a chart like the one above. Think of more interesting sub-headings for the ones you chose in question 4.

How information is organised

Different methods are used to organise information, depending on the type of text and the needs of the reader.

6 Look at the three texts below. For each one decide:
- what it is
- how the information is organised
- why the information is organised in this way.

A

```
BAYLES
BAYLES J.R., 4 Cave Rd Huntingdon................ (01904) 762081
BAYLEY A.S., 14 Wistow Rd Malton................. (01653) 183874
BAYLEY T.R., Valley Farm Warthill................. (01904) 937495
BAYLISH G. H., 2 The Crescent Malton............. (01653) 893732
BAYS S., 28 Holly Bank Rd York................... (01904) 937474
BAYSTON D., 4 Black Smith Lane Asselby........... (01757) 630765
  J., 6 Sandringham Cotts High Hunsley............ (01430) 827456
  M., Pebble House, 140 Beckfield Rd York......... (01904) 837361
BEACH R., 40 Westbourne Grove Goole.............. (01405) 762938
  R. Quarry Bank Cottage North Rd York............ (01904) 358432
  T., 2 Orchard Way Strensall..................... (01904) 837360
BEADLE A., 7 Manor View Pocklington.............. (01759) 938737
  E., 8 Lowfield St Barlby........................ (01757) 893837
  E.M., 23 St. Andrewgate York.................... (01904) 837363
  M., 1 Main St Easingwold........................ (01347) 938373
  N., 8 Derwent Rd Goole.......................... (01405) 838262
  P., 2 The Shrubberies Cliffe.................... (01757) 383737
```

B *[TV listings page]*

C

Mondays to Fridays				HC					NORTHBOUND
London King's Cross	d	1130	1135	1200	1210	1230	1235	1300	1310
Stevenage	d	1150	1154		1229		1257	1246p	
Peterborough	a	1221	1227	1246	1300	1316		1346	1357
Cambridge	d	1104p		1112v	1204p			1233v	
Peterborough	d	1221	1227	1247	1301	1317		1346	1358
Grantham	d		1246		1320		1342		1417
Newark North Gate	a	1250	1258					1355	1429
Lincoln Central	a		1328m				1456m		
Newark North Gate	d	1250	1258					1355	1429
Retford	d				1342				
Doncaster	a	1314			1357	1406	1420	1433	1453
Grimsby Town	a	1444b						1542b	
Hull	a					1507b		1551b	
Doncaster	d	1315			1357	1407	1421	1434	1453
Wakefield Westgate	a		1337		1414		1439		1514
Leeds	a		1355		1435		1501		1535

© National Express. Please note that train times will not be valid.

9 Finding information

Scanning different types of text

Scanning is about using your reading skills to find the correct detail quickly.

7 Scan the texts on page 40 to find the answers to the following questions. Write each answer down. Aim to find all the answers in as short a time as possible.

   a Which channel would you turn to in order to watch *Mastermind*?
   b What time train do you need to catch from Peterborough in order to arrive in Leeds in time for a meeting at 1445?
   c At what time would you turn on for *Wire in the Blood*?
   d What would you find out about in the programme *The American Future*?
   e What code do you dial to contact M. Beadle?
   f What problem is there in contacting R. Beach?
   g If you wanted to end the day with some news, which channel would you turn to?
   h Who lives at 28 Holly Bank Rd?
   i You need to deliver something to a Mr Beadle whose phone number is 01904 837363. What address do you deliver to?
   j On which channel could you watch an episode of *Star Trek*?
   k At what time does the 1135 from King's Cross leave Grantham?
   l How many trains are there daily from Peterborough to Newark North Gate?
   m Which train should you catch to arrive at Leeds at 1501?
   n What different programmes could a family be watching at 8.30pm?
   o Who guest host on *Have I Got News for You*?

Checkpoint

Check your answers to question **7a** to **o** with another student. Where they differ, look back at the text and decide who is right.

Write five more questions of your own based on the texts on page 40. Swap questions and see who is the quickest at finding the correct answers.

Summary

In this unit you have:
- developed your skills in scanning a range of texts
- considered how information is organised in different texts
- used a range of sub-headings.

10 Finding the right answer

In this unit ...
you will study a text and diagrams closely and answer a range of multiple-choice questions on them. You will also sequence and write your own information text.

Information can be presented in many different ways. In this text, the writer uses maps, graphics, a table and a graph, as well as words to give information to the reader. In order to understand the text fully, you need to be able to get the correct information from each of these.

HOW IT RATES A busy market town since the 8th century, Louth is located on the edge of the Lincolnshire Wolds and the banks of the River Lud. It became a major trading area in the 1770s with the construction of a canal. In 1920 the river and canal flooded, wrecking large areas and killing 23 people; the canal was closed in 1924. Today the town is a microcosm of rural life, with open-air street stalls and one of the busiest cattle markets in the country.

QUALITY OF LIFE Pretty good. Louth is a warm and welcoming town, with many shops selling local produce. Hubbard Hills, on the edge of town, is a pretty valley with parkland; the riverside setting makes it a good picnic area. Walking is popular in these parts: the annual walking festival in May–June is a huge event.

POPULATION About 17,000 in the town, with a further 12,000 in the surrounding area. Those aged over 55 comprise more than 40 per cent of the population. Women outnumber men by 700.

TRAVEL A car is vital. There is no railway station – the nearest mainline station is in Grimsby, 14 miles away. The traffic-free roads at least mean that Skegness and Lincoln are both only a short drive away.

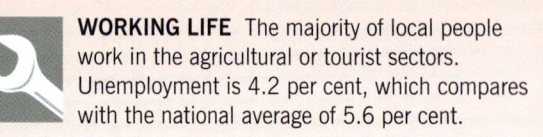

WORKING LIFE The majority of local people work in the agricultural or tourist sectors. Unemployment is 4.2 per cent, which compares with the national average of 5.6 per cent.

UPSIDE This is a true country market town, with local produce and markets every Wednesday, Friday and Saturday. The best way to discover this Area of Outstanding Natural Beauty is on foot.

DOWNSIDE The town may seem a little twee to some people, and it's not exactly the most fashionable county.

Focus on ... LOUTH

Average property prices £000s

	Louth	North Lincs	East Midlands
All properties	165	102	124
Terraced	121	57	71
Semi-detached	144	83	100
Detached	207	137	164
Flats/maisonettes	91	45	61

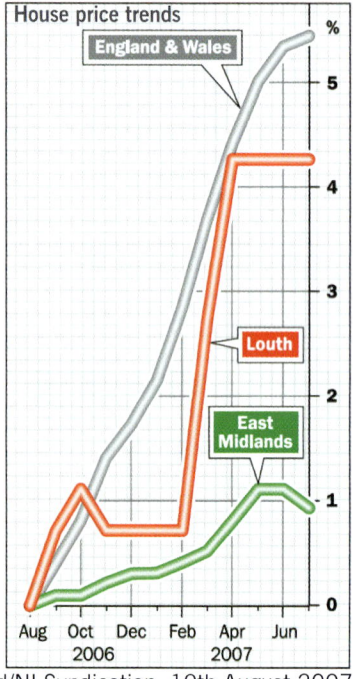

House price trends

© Lorna Blackwood/NI Syndication, 10th August 2007

10 **Finding the right answer**

Reading the text

Part of the information on page 42 is written in paragraphs. Graphics are used to:
- help the reader quickly identify the subject of each paragraph
- make the text look more interesting.

Read the information in the paragraphs on page 42 closely before answering the following questions. Your answers should be based only on what you have read. Each question gives you four possible answers but only one of these is correct.

1 Unemployment in Louth is:
   a greater than the national average
   b caused by the local tourist sector
   c lower than the national average
   d highest in the farming community.

2 Many of the shops in Louth:
   a are very expensive   **b** sell walking equipment
   c are on the edge of town   **d** sell local produce.

3 If you move to Louth it is vital that you:
   a work in tourism or agriculture   **b** have a car
   c enjoy walking   **d** are aged over 55.

Reading the maps

The map and inset are included in the article on page 42 to:
- give the reader information that could not easily be given in words
- make the page look more interesting.

Study the map and the inset on page 42 closely before answering the following questions. Your answers should be based on the map and inset only. Remember, there is only one correct answer for each question.

4 To get from Louth to Coningsby you would take the:
   a A16   **b** A157   **c** A631   **d** A153.

5 The distance between Louth and Lincoln in miles is approximately:
   a 0–10 miles   **b** 10–20 miles   **c** 20–30 miles   **d** 30–40 miles.

6 Louth is on:
   a the east coast of England   **b** the west coast of England
   c the south coast of England   **d** the south-east coast of England.

Reading the table and graph

The table and graph are included in the text to:
- give the reader information that could not easily be given in words
- make the page look more interesting.

Study the table and graph on page 42 closely before answering the following questions. Your answers should be based on the table and graph only.

7 Which of the following statements is true?
   a Properties are more expensive in Louth than in the East Midlands.
   b A semi-detached house in North Lincolnshire will cost you more than one in the East Midlands.
   c A terraced house in North Lincolnshire is the cheapest property you can buy.
   d A detached house in Louth costs twice as much as one in North Lincolnshire.

English: The Basic Skills

8 Which of the following statements is true?
  a House prices have stayed the same in the East Midlands since August 2006.
  b House prices rose rapidly between February and April 2007 in Louth.
  c There has been a steady drop in the price of houses in England and Wales.
  d House prices have risen less quickly in Louth than in the East Midlands.

9 Which of the following statements is **not** true?
  a The average price of a terraced house in Louth is £121,000.
  b House prices rose steadily in England and Wales between August 2006 and June 2007.
  c A detached house in the East Midlands costs more than one in North Lincolnshire.
  d Property is cheaper in Louth than in the East Midlands.

Checkpoint

Check your answers to questions 1–9 with a partner. Where you disagree, re-read the text and various illustrations and decide who is right.

Try to work out why the wrong answer was given to avoid making the same mistake again in the future.

Drawing conclusions

You have read the text and diagrams closely and answered questions on them. You are now ready to move onto the next stage in developing your reading skills. To do this you need to make conclusions about content, purpose and audience based on the details in the text.

The following questions test how well you have understood what you have read. As before, there is only one correct answer for each question.

10 The main purpose of the text on page 42 is to:
  a attract tourists to the area
  b criticise transport in Louth
  c give information about Louth
  d show the good things about Louth.

11 Louth might be a good place to buy a house if:
  a you like city life
  b you enjoy walking
  c you have a canal boat
  d you cannot drive.

10 **Finding the right answer**

12 The average property prices table would be helpful to:
  a people who want to rent a house
  b people who want to live near the sea
  c people who want a good quality of life
  d people who want to compare house prices in the area.

Checkpoint

Check your answers to questions 10–12 with a partner. Where you disagree, re-read the text and decide who is right. Try to work out why the wrong answer was given to avoid making the same mistake again in the future.

Writing for purpose and audience

The text on page 42 is written for people who might be thinking of buying a house there (audience). It aims to inform them about the place and to give information on house prices (purpose).

13 You are going to write two informative paragraphs about the place where you live, for people who might be thinking of moving there. Your aim is to inform your readers about the place's 'upside' and 'downside'. Follow these steps:

  A List between three and five *positive* points about the place and between three and five *negative* points about the place.

  Your points might be to do with:
  - the surrounding area
  - the local shops and schools
  - things to do in the place.
  - transport
  - the people

  B Decide on the best order in which to make your points.

  C Write two paragraphs. Each paragraph should contain about five sentences. Use sub-headings: 'Upside' for your first paragraph and 'Downside' for your second paragraph. Aim to make your points clearly.

  D When you have finished your writing, check that:
  - you have given your reader relevant information
  - your paragraphs are clear and well organised
  - your spelling and punctuation are accurate.

Summary

In this unit you have:
- studied a text of more than one paragraph including maps, a table, graphics and a graph
- obtained specific information through detailed reading
- made conclusions based on the text
- written a clear and well-organised text suitable for your purpose and audience.

11 Meet and eat

Meet and eat
Employment Application Form

Please use block capitals.

Position applied for:

Crew member ☐   Customer care operative ☐   Other _____

Personal details:

Forename(s) _____   Surname _____

Address _____

_____   Postcode _____

Home tel. _____   Mobile _____

E-mail address _____   National Insurance no. _____

Have you ever worked in a restaurant before?   Yes ☐   No ☐

Next of kin:

Name _____   Relationship _____

Address _____

_____   Postcode _____

Home tel. _____

Present and previous employment:

Employment dates	Employer's name and address	Job title and responsibilities	Reason(s) for leaving

Secondary education and training:

Dates from / to	School / College	Exams / Awards

11 **Meet and eat**

In this unit ...
you will read and fill in an application form and write a letter of application.

Many young people have part-time jobs outside school or college. Read the first part of the application form for the fictional restaurant **Meet and eat** which appears on the opposite page. This contains many of the kinds of questions you could be asked when applying for various part-time jobs.

Giving the required details

When applying for a job, it is important to make a good first impression. The application form is the first filter for employers.

1 Make a rough copy of what you would write in the spaces of the application form opposite. Use the following prompts to help you.

Block capitals This means you have to write in capital letters.

Position applied for As this is a job for a crew member, you would tick this space. If it were a different job, you would tick customer care operative or write the job title next to 'other'.

Personal details If you do not have a mobile number, e-mail address or National Insurance number, write N/A, which stands for 'Not Applicable'.

Next of kin Employers usually want this information in case they need to contact a relative in a case of emergency. It is normal to give the name of a parent or guardian or a close relative.

Present and previous employment If you have had previous jobs write them here, starting with your most recent one. If not, write N/A in the first column.

Secondary education and training Start with the school or college you are attending now. Give the results of any exams you have taken, including GCSEs. If you haven't taken any exams yet then list the results of your KS3 tests instead. Also name any awards you have received in school, such as attendance and effort awards or sports medals. If you have attended any other secondary schools or colleges list them here also.

2 Check the details carefully. Correct any mistakes in spelling and the use of capital letters, and make sure everything will fit into the spaces provided.

3 Now copy the first page of the application form from page 46 (or you may be given a copy) and fill it in using your neatest handwriting. The final copy, the one the employer sees, should be perfect.

English: The Basic Skills

Looking at a range of responses

Employers sometimes want to find out a bit about you before they decide to interview you. They will often ask specific questions on application forms to help them to do this. If you want a job, it is important to think about what your employer is looking for.

4 a This application is for the position of crew member in a restaurant. Make a list of the qualities you think this employer would be looking for.

b Read the 'About you' section of the application form on the right. This requires a detailed answer. Read the first drafts of three students' responses to this below.

About you:
What do you like doing in your spare time? Include any interests or hobbies.

In my spare time I like to go fishing with my mates we go to Barthwick Lakes just about every weekend because there are allot off fish their. Some Mondays I go to the youth club on are estate, but I havent been lately because I have got allot of coursework to do. On a friday night I go out with my mates and we hang around our estate drinking.
— James

Homework, homework and homework are the three things which actually take up most of what spare time I have. However, in those brief moments when I do have some spare time from school work, what I really like doing is playing football. Yes, you read it correctly, a girl who likes playing football! I play for my local U16 7-a-side team which has been together since primary school. I find that physical exercise and working together as a team both help me to cope with my schoolwork. I now feel that I need to use these skills in a place of work.
— Chantelle

Most of my spare time is taken up with my friends. They are important to me because they are always there for me when I need them. One of my friends mums has been very ill recently and we have been helping her by taking her out. I also spend a lot of time on the sunbeds as well as looking after my younger brothers and sisiters.
— Charlotte

Pair activity

5 With a partner, read and assess each of these responses using the following descriptors.

1. Answers the question, interesting and organised, accurate and needs no corrections.
2. Mostly answers the question, usually interesting and organised, needs some corrections.
3. Attempts to answer the question, some relevant content, needs many corrections.

Think about your answer to activity 4a. With your partner, write two points of advice for each of these students on how they could improve their first drafts.

11 **Meet and eat**

Writing your own responses

When writing answers in application forms it is important to make sure you:

- answer the question that was asked
- organise your answer
- make it interesting
- check your grammar, spelling and punctuation are accurate.

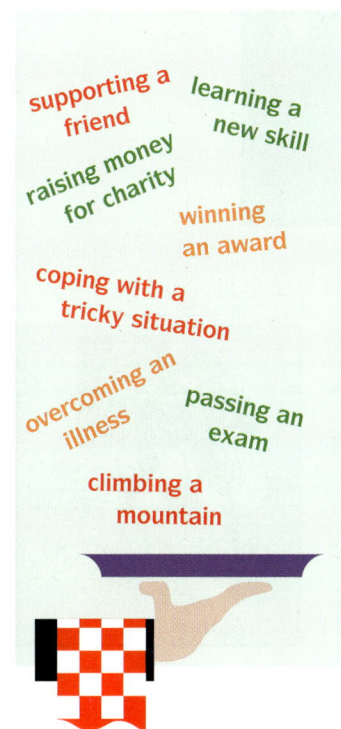

6 You are going to draft an answer to the next question on the application form:

What do you think is your greatest achievement to date? Explain why.

Follow these steps:

- Choose something appropriate. On the left are some prompts to help you.
- Once you have made your choice, write a list of the main points you want to make. Remember, the question asks you to explain why this is your greatest achievement.
- Draft your answer. Aim to write about 100 words.

supporting a friend
learning a new skill
raising money for charity
winning an award
coping with a tricky situation
overcoming an illness
passing an exam
climbing a mountain

Checkpoint

When you have finished your draft:
- Read it as though you were the employer. Would you want to interview this person to work in your restaurant? Make any changes to your draft that you feel will help your application.
- Ask a partner to read your draft and comment on
  - the content and organisation
  - the accuracy of your punctuation, grammar and spelling.

7 Write your final draft, making any helpful changes. Make sure you present your final draft neatly.

Summary

In this unit you have:
- read and understood an application form
- assessed sample responses
- presented information accurately and clearly
- used detail appropriate to your purpose and audience.

49

12 Phones at work

In this unit …
you will learn how to develop an appropriate phone manner for different situations and how to deal with a range of callers effectively.

Using a phone is an essential skill in life. You need to learn to adapt what you say and how you say it according to the purpose of the call and the person you are speaking to.

It needs a full service.

Extensions on Saturday?

Yes, the students' results are excellent.

How many rooms are required?

It's still painful?

Try to stay calm.

They're entering the shop now.

Yes, I've got the paint you wanted.

12 Phones at work

It's for you

For many people, phone conversations are part of their daily work. It is important that they deal with callers courteously and efficiently and make sure, whenever possible, that their queries are answered.

1 Look at the images of people at work on page 50. Identify:
- the job each person appears to be doing
- the reason(s) why they might need to take phone calls at work.

2 List three other jobs where a worker may need to take phone calls and the type of calls they would need to deal with.

How to speak to callers

Many organisations and companies issue guidelines to their staff on how to answer the phone most effectively. The following guidelines were written for reception staff answering the phone in a college. Read them closely before answering the questions below.

Constance Maths and Technology College
GUIDELINES FOR EFFECTIVE PHONE SERVICE

1. Answer calls promptly, by the second or third ring.
2. Greet all callers with 'Good morning' or 'Good afternoon' and the college name.
3. Ask how you can help the caller.
4. Listen attentively, and take notes, if needed. Restate important points of information to check understanding and accuracy.
5. Always speak in standard English.
6. Speak clearly, controlling your volume and speed.
7. Avoid talking with anything in your mouth, such as chewing gum.
8. Ask the caller if you may put him/her on hold if you need to speak to another staff member about the call, or need to check any information.
9. Make sure you follow the correct procedures for taking messages or transferring calls to a staff member's voicemail.
10. If a caller is upset or difficult, stay calm and polite and refer the call to a senior member of staff.
11. When calls cannot be dealt with immediately, always agree with the caller a date and time when they can be contacted again.

3 Answer these questions to check you have understood the guidelines.
- **a** How should you check understanding and accuracy?
- **b** What should you do if you need to speak to another member of staff?
- **c** How should you greet all callers?
- **d** How soon should you answer calls?
- **e** What should you do if the caller is upset or difficult
- **f** What should you do if a call cannot be dealt with immediately?
- **g** What should you avoid doing when answering the phone?

English: The Basic Skills

Speaking in standard English

The guidelines recommend that people taking calls should always speak in standard English. Standard English is the way the language is spoken in more formal situations across the country.

4 Copy the following table. The phrases in the first column are non-standard English. Decide and write down a more appropriate standard English form that would carry the same meaning. The first one has been done for you.

Non-standard English	Standard English
He's a right little monkey …	He can be very mischievous.
Hang on a minute …	
She was all over the place …	
Yeah … well … that's just the way it is these days …	
Well, he couldn't of handed it in here …	

Checkpoint

Check your answers to question 3 with a partner. Are there any other rules you think are important that should be added to the list of guidelines? If there are, write them down.

Check your answers to 4 with a partner. Decide which of you has chosen the most appropriate standard English alternatives.

Improving your phone manner

You are now going to work with a partner to prepare yourselves to answer phone calls at college. The aim is to improve your phone manner together.

Pair activity

5 a With your partner, decide on the first things you will say when you pick up the phone. Remember the guidelines:

- Greet all callers with 'Good morning' or 'Good afternoon' and the college name.
- Ask how you can help the caller.

b Write down the exact words you will use.

c Practise this with your partner, each taking turns to answer the phone, and remembering to:

- Always speak in standard English.
- Speak clearly, controlling your volume and speed.
- Avoid talking with anything in your mouth, such as chewing gum.

12 **Phones at work**

Dealing with calls

Remember, when dealing with callers your job is to help them. You should remain calm and polite at all times.

Pair activity

6 You are now going to be presented with several different situations that the college receptionists may have to deal with when answering the phone.

a Below are a few details about the callers and the first thing they each say. Read them carefully.

b Take it in turns to be the caller and a receptionist.

c Improvise the rest of the conversation. Remember that the receptionist should be following the college guidelines given on page 51.

'Good morning, I wonder whether you could help me? I'm hoping to take my family on holiday and need to know when February half-term is next year.'

'No, it's not a good morning! I'm sick of the lazy louts from your place taking a short cut over my front garden. I've phoned up several times before and now I've had enough!'

'Oh, hello there. I wonder whether you could advise me on which form I need to apply for an energy saving grant for my home improvements?'

'Good afternoon. This is James Clayton from the 21st Century Drama Group. We're currently visiting your area and I wondered if you would be interested in making a booking?'

Checkpoint

In your pair, decide which situation each of you best handled in the role of receptionist. Identify the things you did well and the things you could further improve. Remember to think about:

- what you said
- how you said it.

Having experimented with answering calls, decide which three rules from the list are the most important. Write them down and explain why you have chosen them.

Summary

In this unit you have:

- considered why people may need to answer the phone at work
- studied and followed some guidelines for effective phone service
- responded appropriately to a caller's needs in a range of situations.

13 Writing a report

BBC Director General's report

The BBC is living between two worlds: the world of traditional radio and television broadcasting and the dizzying new world of digital media. Our challenge is to strike the right balance of resources and creative energy between these two worlds and to set the right pace of change.

2005/2006 was a year in which the digital revolution shifted up another gear. Month after month, the BBC's website set new records for reach. Live streaming, downloads, podcasts…

A

18th April 1875

I was on duty at Blunham on Saturday April 17th between six and seven in the evening. I was called to the Salutation public house kept by Charles Howard. I went in the house and found a man named Thomas Pestell of Whyboston. He was drunk and said he had lost his purse and sixty pounds which he said someone had stolen. I told him to search his clothes and he said you may search them yourself. I did so and found the purse and money in his trousers leg. I told him he had better go home at once…

B

Charlene has potential and, on occasion, produces work of a high standard. She does not, however, always give her full attention to her studies and is easily distracted in class. Occasionally, homework is not completed and she is behind with her coursework assignments.

With a little more effort and a little less chatter she could do well in her forthcoming exams.

C

England slump to defeat

By TONI LANE
December 05, 2006

An England batting collapse led to an unexpected second Test loss in Adelaide and a 2-0 series lead for Australia.

Resuming the final day at the Adelaide Oval 97 runs ahead on 59 for one, England knew that a solid batting performance would all but end Australia's slim hopes of claiming victory.

But just as the tourists seemed to have weathered the early pressure, they lost nine wickets for 70 runs to be dismissed for 129.

And Australia, chasing a victory target of 168, sealed victory by reaching the total for the loss of four wickets with 19 balls remaining.

D

HOMEBUYER REPORT

23, Fantasy Drive

A: INTRODUCTION

Please note that this Report is solely for your use and your professional advisers' and no liability to anyone else is accepted. Should you not act upon specific, reasonable advice contained in this Report, no responsibility is accepted for the consequences.

Objective

The principal objective of the Report and Valuation is to assist you to:

- Make a reasoned and informed judgement on whether or not to proceed with the purchase
- Assess whether or not …

E

A © BBC, B © Hooper & Fletcher archive – report by police constable Thomas Stock of an incident at the public house on 18th April 1875, E © TheMoveChannel

13 Writing a report

In this unit ...
you will read and understand a range of reports and write a report including an appropriate level of detail and using the correct tense.

There are many different kinds of report. Some examples are given on page 54.

Report writing at work

There are many jobs in which the ability to write a clear report is a required skill. Look at report E opposite, for example. Surveyors must write clear and accurate reports to enable people to choose the right house.

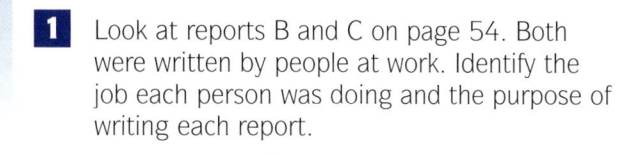

1 Look at reports B and C on page 54. Both were written by people at work. Identify the job each person was doing and the purpose of writing each report.

Pair activity

2 With another student, list the reasons why the following people might have to write reports as part of their work: doctors, personal trainers, mechanics, journalists and care assistants.

Tenses

The main tenses used in reports are past and present. For example:

Rising damp was discovered on all downstairs walls ...
(past tense)

Mr Gray is suffering from a rare disorder that requires...
(present tense)

3 Look again at the reports on page 54.
  a Which reports are written entirely in the past tense?
  b Explain why the past tense is used in these reports.
  c Which reports are written entirely in the present tense?
  d Explain why the present tense is used in these reports.
  e Which report uses both the past and present tenses?
  f Explain why both tenses are used in this report.

4 It is important to use tenses correctly. The writer of the following report, 'For Sale', has got his tenses mixed up. Read the report carefully and copy the words where the tense is incorrect. Write the correct words next to them.

FOR SALE

This property is constructed in 2001 and occupied a quiet position on the edge of this central development and within walking distance of the city. Situated on three floors, the house offered three bedrooms, two living areas, a kitchen and two bathrooms. The main living room had spectacular open views across Bootham Park and the kitchen is recently refurbished with extensive oak fitments and breakfast bar. A garage and charming front and back gardens will complete the picture of this very desirable property.

5 Imagine your house, or one you know well, is up for sale. Write the estate agent's 'For Sale' report. Use the example given above to help you. Make sure you use the past and present tenses correctly.

English: The Basic Skills

Selection of detail

When writers report on a football match they don't give a second-by-second account of the game – it would be a ridiculously long report. Writers have to select the main points in the match, the ones the reader would be interested in, and report these.

Similarly when teachers write reports on students, they don't write everything they know about those students. They select the things that are relevant to the subject and what the students' parents or guardians would want to know.

Jodie's English teacher knows the following things about her and is about to write her end-of-year report.

- bites her nails
- has a tattoo on her left wrist
- sits next to Caitlin
- is nearly always cheerful
- her first homework was too short
- has brown hair with red highlights
- should get a good grade in her English exam
- finds it difficult to join in with group discussion
- was late to class on November 8th
- handwriting is better when she uses a pen
- laughed out loud at Mark's joke last week
- looked tired one Monday morning
- has completed her coursework assignments
- loved the poem we read today
- finds Shakespeare difficult
- likes Craig a little more than she should

Pair activity

6 In pairs:
- make a list of the things the teacher might use in a report
- place these in order of importance
- write a report on Jodie that is no more than 100 words. Write mainly in the present tense and make sure you have included the most important things for an English teacher.

Checkpoint

Swap reports with another pair. Check that the report:
- includes the details on Jodie that are most relevant to an English teacher's report
- is written mainly in the present tense
- is clear and accurate.

Feed back to the other pair on how well they have done on each of the bullet points.

13 Writing a report

Different formats for reports

In a report the writer gives information to the reader. This can be presented in a number of different ways – through prose, graphs, tables, diagrams and charts.

7 a Read the following extract from an online AA report on the Mini Cooper.

Ratings

Overall Rating	●●●●●●●●○
Value for money	●●●●●●○○○
Costs	●●●●●●●○○
Space and practicality	●●●●●○○○○
Controls and display	●●●●●●○○○
Comfort	●●●●●●●○○
Security	●●●●●●○○○
Safety	●●●●●●○○○

Likes
☺ 'Must have' image appeals to everybody and offends no one.
☺ BMW levels of build quality make the Mini ultra reliable.
☺ Bulletproof image means that depreciation is kept to a minimum.
☺ Fabled Mini handling will keep your inner boy racer satisfied.

Gripes
☹ Too much equipment is left on options list, which forces up real cost.
☹ Lack of rear passenger room severely hinders practicality.
☹ Some interior trim feels plasticky and a little cheap.
☹ Cooper's levels of performance don't seem to merit price tag.

Our Verdict
The coolest car on the planet gets even cooler with a 'Cooper' badge.

© The AA

Everybody loves the Mini's cute face

b Think about the way this report is presented. Copy the following table and list the advantages and disadvantages of this report.

Advantages	Disadvantages

8 Use your imagination to create a similar kind of report. It needs to be on something you know about. This could be a car, bike, shop, magazine, place or something else. Make up your own headings for the ratings table to suit your chosen subject and include your own **Likes** and **Gripes**.

Summary

In this unit you have:
- recognised that report writing is an essential part of many jobs
- examined the correct uses of tenses in reports
- selected the main points for a report
- assessed the effectiveness of an online report
- written three different kinds of report.

57

14 A sporting chance

In this unit ...
you will read and respond to different texts and present information on a complex subject logically and clearly.

Many people need to deal with the public in their work. It is their job to deal with the post, e-mails and voicemails.

Responding to different texts

Imagine you work in a leisure centre and have to deal with the following communications from members of the public. Think about each one carefully before deciding on the best course of action. Then answer the questions that follow.

> Dear Sir/Madam,
>
> I visited your pool last week and was impressed with the new facilities that have recently been installed. I was horrified, however, to discover that the temperature of the pool was well below what I would have expected. I could only stay in the water for 10 minutes and even then I was blue when I came out.
>
> Unless this situation improves, I shall not be returning to your pool.
>
> Yours faithfully,
>
> Mr C Lawton

1 Which of the following do you think would be the most appropriate action to take? Explain why.
   a Write back saying that notices of the low temperature were posted around the pool and changing rooms.
   b Write back explaining that there was a problem and that this has now been fixed.
   c Write back explaining that there was a problem but it is now fixed and enclose a voucher for a free swim.
   d File the letter and wait to see if Mr Lawton writes again.

2 Study the e-mail message at the top of the next page. Which of the following do you think would be the most appropriate action to take? Explain why.
   a E-mail Imran asking what kind of event he wants to have and how much he wants to pay.
   b E-mail Imran asking for an address to which you can send the *Kids' Parties* brochure.
   c Scan the *Kid's Parties* brochure and e-mail it to Imran.
   d E-mail Imran asking him to ring you for more details.

14 A sporting chance

> I'm wanting to find a suitable venue for a party for my six year old and I understand that the leisure centre runs different kinds of events. I wonder if you could tell me what you do and how much it would cost me?
>
> Thank you,
>
> Imran Khan

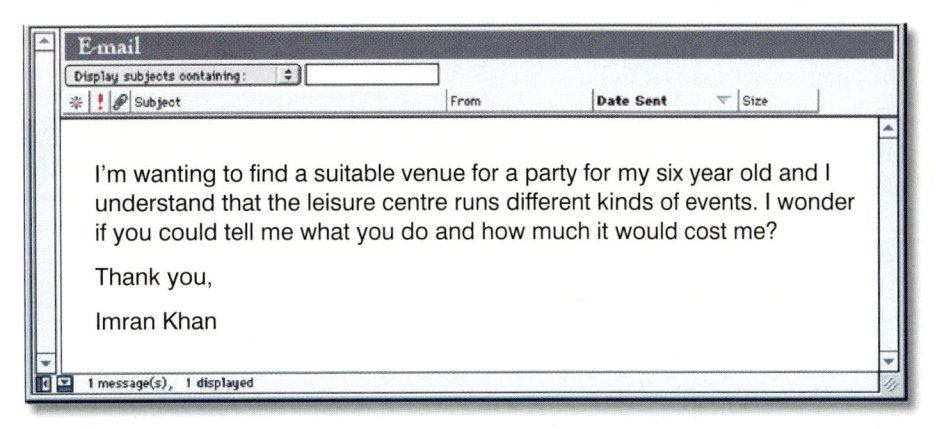

LEISURE CENTRE

Our aim is to make our customers happy. If you are not satisfied with any part of our service, please complete this card giving details and we will get back to you.

Name: Sarah Mapleton   Tel no. 0121 745 8888

Comment: The changing rooms were filthy and looked as though they hadn't been properly cleaned for days. I couldn't put my toddler, Ben, down on the floor in case he picked up some bit of rubbish. Not at all a happy customer.

Date: 12/04/08   Signature: S Mapleton

3 Which of the following do you think would be the most appropriate action to take first after reading the comment slip above? Explain why.
  a Ring Sarah Mapleton, apologising for the state of the changing rooms and promising that the complaint will be looked into.
  b Find out why the changing rooms had not been properly cleaned.
  c Show the complaint to the cleaners.
  d Show the complaint to the manager of the centre.

VOICEMAIL 4
'Hello. My name is Katie Flintoff. I'm a student at the local college and am hoping to get some work over the summer holidays. Can you tell me if there are any vacancies at the leisure centre for either part-time or full-time work? My number is 01267 889650.'

4 Which of the following do you think would be the most appropriate action to take first? Explain why.
  a Ring Katie Flintoff and invite her to come in for an interview.
  b Ignore the call and wait for Katie to ring again.
  c Ask the manager of the leisure centre if there are any vacancies.
  d Ring Katie and tell her there are no vacancies at the moment.

5 List the extra details you need in order to help this caller.

Explain why you need these details.

VOICEMAIL 5
'Hello. I was at the leisure centre last week with my three children and I think I left one of their swimming costumes behind. Could you let me know if it was found? Thanks now.'

Checkpoint

Discuss the choices and reasons you gave in your answers to questions 1–5 with another student. Decide which of you made the best choices and why. If you need to, make changes to the choices you made.

English: The Basic Skills

How complex material is presented

People in all kinds of service industries may have studied for a long time in order to become qualified. They need to let members of the public know what they do, and how they can be of service, in words that can be easily understood. To do this, they need to present a range of complex ideas in a straightforward, clear and 'user-friendly' form.

6 The following extract is taken from a leaflet in which the writer is informing the reader of how he or she could benefit from sports and remedial massage therapy. He has used a number of devices to help present complex information clearly. Read the extracts closely.

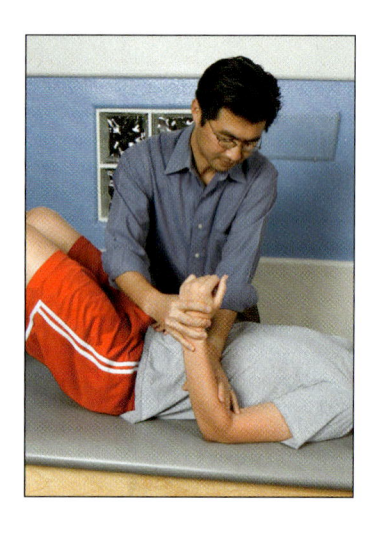

Identify and write down an example of each of the following:

- A sub-heading to organise information
- B rhetorical question to reflect what the reader might be thinking
- C use of 'our' to give a sense of shared experience
- D personal pronoun 'you' to challenge the reader directly
- E easy-to-understand definition of sports massage therapy
- F examples to show the kind of people who would benefit from the therapy
- G simple checklist to help the reader understand
- H bold print to highlight key points
- I bullet points to itemise key pieces of information.

What is Sport & Remedial Massage?

Sports Massage Therapy is the manipulation and assessment of soft tissue such as muscles, tendons and ligaments. The treatments are designed and tailored to suit the individual client, regardless of his or her athletic ability.

Its primary function should lie in injury prevention by reducing tension, improving flexibility, range of movement and by improving the circulation and general well-being of the client. Instead of using our 'ability' to carry on with the help of drugs and putting up with the discomfort, Sports Massage Therapy can be used to restore muscle function, strength and flexibility through the breakdown of scar tissue and adhesions.

Anyone and everyone can benefit from Massage Therapy, from world-class athletes to the weekend gardener.

Could You Benefit From Sports Massage?

If you have aches and pains in any of the following areas then the answer would be **YES**!

✓ Neck ✓ Shoulder ✓ Chest ✓ Arm (any part)
✓ Leg (any part) ✓ Ankle ✓ Foot

Benefits of Sports Massage

- **Maintains the entire body in a better physical condition** – improving the circulation of blood and lymph i.e. nutrients in and waste products out

- **Extends the good health and general life of your athletic career** – quicker recovery from injury whilst reducing the chance of re-injury

- **Boosts athletic performance and endurance** – reduces muscle soreness, resulting in consistently higher levels of training

- **Prevents injury and loss of mobility to muscle** – promotes flexibility and relaxation whilst improving muscle tone

- **Cures and restores mobility to injured muscle** – adhesions and scar tissue can be broken down, giving back the muscles' structural integrity and flexibility.

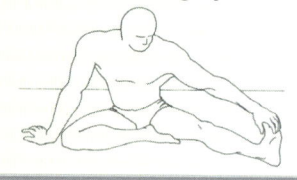

14 A sporting chance

Presenting complex material clearly

As the text on sports massage shows, when presenting complex material it helps to:

- break it down into smaller sections
- use a range of devices to inform and involve your reader.

7 Choose a sport that you know about and think other people might be interested in. You are going to write about it in a way that:
- presents complex information clearly
- interests your reader
- shows the reader the benefits of taking part in the sport.

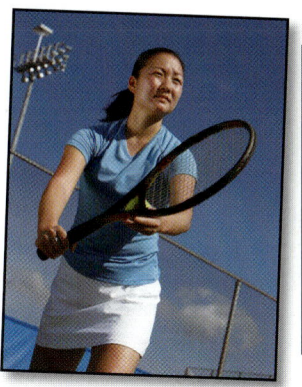

Follow stages A to E.

A Make notes detailing everything you know about your chosen sport. You could make a list, or lay your ideas out in a spidergram.

B Group or colour-code your notes under the following three headings:

What is …?   Could you benefit from …?   Benefits of …

C Under the first heading, write a clear explanation of what the sport is and what it involves.

D Under the second heading, make a checklist to show the reader the benefits of taking part in the sport.

E Under the third heading, list the benefits of the sport.

Checkpoint

Compare your writing with that of another two or three students. Decide whether you have:
- presented complex information clearly
- used devices to interest your reader.

Summary

In this unit you have:
- responded actively to different texts
- investigated how complex material is presented clearly
- presented complex material clearly and logically using a range of devices.

61

15 Read, respond, go

Application for a driving licence
Please read booklet INF1D when filling in this form.

D1

In this unit ...
you will read and follow instructions to help you complete parts of a driving licence application form.

You can apply for a driving licence online at www.dvla.gov.uk or using a hard copy. It is important to fill in the form correctly. If you do not, your application will be delayed and the form may be returned to you.

To fill in forms correctly, you need to read the instructions closely and follow them exactly.

Reading instructions closely

Many forms come with detailed instructions which tell you how to fill in the form correctly. The form for application for a driving licence D1 comes with a booklet (INF1D).

The booklet takes you through the sections of the application form and explains what you need to do.

1 Read closely the following instructions from the booklet INF1D which are given to help you complete Section 1 of the application form. Then answer the questions that follow them.

Section 1 – Your current details

Please fill in the relevant parts of this section.

The address on the licence must be a residential one. We do not accept PO Box Number addresses.

Change of name or address

If your name or address (or both) has changed since your last licence was issued, please enter your **new and old** details in section 1. Proof of name change will be needed – see Section 6 for details.

You must also provide your current paper driving licence or, if you have a photocard licence, please return the photocard and the counterpart. If you have lost either part, you will need to apply for a replacement licence. The fee for this is shown on the D1 form.

It is a legal requirement that you tell DVLA immediately of any change to your permanent address in GB. The offence of failure to notify carries a fine of up to £1000. If you have advised DVLA of any changes and sent in your old-style paper licence, you must make a qualifying application for a licence with change of personal details.

a What kind of address is not accepted?
b Which section should you turn to for more details on change of name?
c What must you do if you change your address?
d What could happen if you fail to notify DVLA of your change of address?

15 **Read, respond, go**

2 Now copy and correctly complete the 'Your current details' section below, which is taken from the driving licence application form. Remember to follow the instructions you read closely in question 1.

2 Your details

Your GB driver number (if you know it):

Title: Mr   Mrs   Miss   Ms   Other (for example, Dr)

Surname:

First names:

Date of birth: DD MM YYYY

Full current address

House No.

Postcode

Checkpoint

Swap your work with another student.
- Check their answers to questions **a** to **d**. If you have different answers, re-read the instructions to find out who is correct.
- Check their completion of the 'Your current details' section. Have they used block capitals, used black ink, filled in all the relevant parts correctly?

Correct any errors in your own work before moving on.

Your photograph

Some forms require you to send a photograph. The instructions will tell you what this photograph must be like.

3 **a** Read the following instructions taken from the DVLA booklet INF1D.

Your photograph

Your photograph must be a recent:
- colour passport style and size (45 millimetres x 35 millimetres)
- a true likeness, showing your full face, with no hat, helmet or sunglasses, although you may wear everyday glasses
- taken against a plain, evenly-lit and light background, and
- signed on the back by the person who has signed section 6 Part C (if this applies).

Please make sure that you send a good-quality colour photograph as we will electronically scan, reduce and copy your photograph onto your photocard driving licence.

Please note the image on your licence will be black and white.

We will accept digital photographs, providing they meet the above criteria.

We will not accept black and white photographs or those that do not meet the requirements above.

English: The Basic Skills

b Below are eight photographs of the same person. Only one of these is acceptable to the DVLA. With a partner, match the annotations to the unsuitable photographs and decide which one is the acceptable photograph.

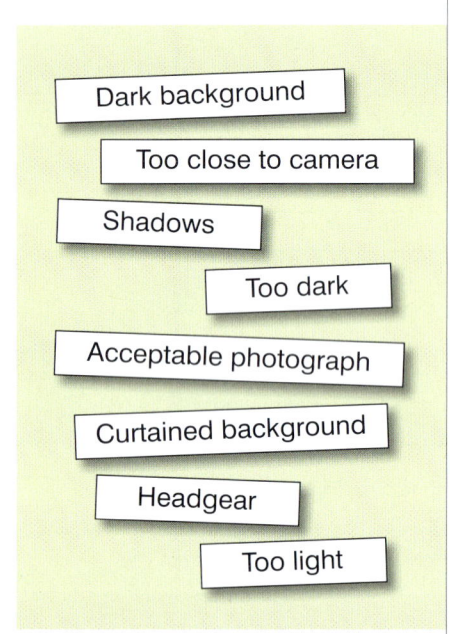

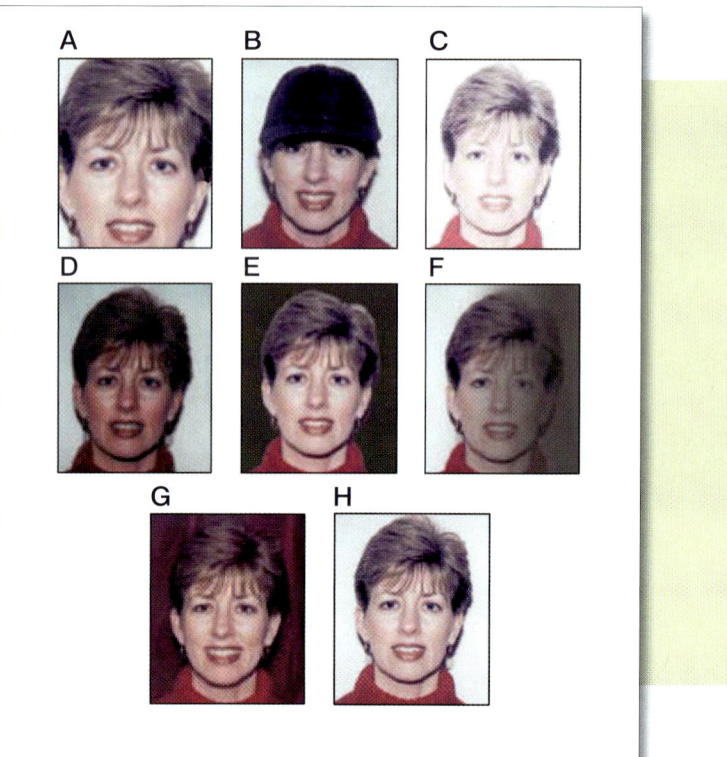

Dark background

Too close to camera

Shadows

Too dark

Acceptable photograph

Curtained background

Headgear

Too light

Signing a form

Never sign a form, or any other document, without reading it closely to be sure of what you are signing. Your signature is a legal commitment and you are responsible for it. You will not escape court action by saying you didn't know what you were signing. It is your responsibility to know.

4 Read the information on the left and following instructions taken from page 13 of the DVLA booklet INF1D. Then answer a–e.

Section 7 – Your signature

Read the declaration and sign the form in **black ink,** making sure that the signature is completely in the white area.

Example of a signature we would not accept:

• Keep your signature within the white box •
A. Sample
• Keep your signature within the white box •   ✗

Example of a signature we would accept:

• Keep your signature within the white box •
A. Sample
• Keep your signature within the white box •   ✓

64

15 **Read, respond, go**

7 Your signature

I declare that I am resident in the UK and understand that it is a criminal offence to make a false declaration to get a driving licence and that to do so can lead to prosecution and a maximum penalty of up to two years imprisonment. I also understand that failing to provide information is an offence that could lead to prosecution and a fine of up to £1000.

Important
See page 13 of INF1D

Date

We will not accept this application unless you sign below in black ink and your signature is completely within the white box.

• Keep your signature within the white box •

• Keep your signature within the white box •

a What exactly are you declaring if you sign this form?

b How might you be punished if you make a false declaration?

c How might you be punished if you fail to provide information?

d What two things do you need to make sure of when you sign your name in the white box?

e Explain why you should always read forms and documents closely before signing them.

Checkpoint

Look back through the work you have done in this unit. Write a list of advice points for people who are about to fill in an application form for a driving licence. Your advice may include general and/or specific points.

Summary

In this unit you have:

- read closely and followed instructions
- completed parts of a driving licence application form
- recognised the importance of signing a form
- given advice on what to do when completing a driving licence application form.

Extracts from the DVLA form D1 and booklet INF1D reprinted with the kind permission of the DVLA. Please note the PDFs and application forms are constantly being updated. Updated information can be found on the DVLA website.

65

16 Organising your day

MEMO

To: Sam
From: Pete
Date: Tuesday 3rd March

Can you attend a meeting in my room at 10.30 to discuss the price changes? It should take no more than 45 minutes. E-mail me with your answer.

Pete

Don't forget. Gran's coming for tea tonight. Said you'd be there ... please. Mum X

Cu 4 lunch @ 12.30 2day? Toni

Did u c match? Wot a wste of tme! ☹
B in café at 6?
Terry

From: "VinceM"
To: <samj@edusupplies4U.com>
Sent: 3 March   08.15
Subject: Health & Safety Meeting

Hi Sam,
Have to delay meeting. Important client coming in. Sorry about that. How about later — around 4.30? Should only take 30 minutes. If I don't hear from you, I'll assume that's okay.
Vince

From: "ChrisH"
To: <samj@edusupplies4U.com>
Sent: 3 March   08.45
Subject: invoices

Sam,
Need to talk to you as a matter of urgency <u>before</u> you complete invoice to Woodfield School.
Chris H

From: "Exerbooks"
To: <samj@edusupplies4U.com>
Sent: 3 March   08.55
Subject: Missing order

Dear Sam,
Re: your enquiry about the missing exercise books. We think we have located the missing parcels and I will get in touch with you later this morning.
Yours,
Trevor Sinclair

16 Organising your day

In this unit ...
you will role play the start of a working day for a clerical officer in an educational supplies company. You will read and listen to a range of messages and respond appropriately to them.

Many people in work start the day by dealing with a range of written and spoken communications. In this unit, your working day is 9 am to 5 pm with one hour for lunch. When you arrive at work on Tuesday 3 March you have a memo, three text messages and three e-mails to respond to. These are on the opposite page. Read them carefully before moving on to the activities below.

Planning your diary

At work it is important to keep your diary updated so that you manage to get everything done and don't double-book appointments.

1 The following is the page of your diary for Tuesday 3 March.
   a Copy this page.
   b In response to your memo, texts and e-mails on page 66, make any necessary changes to your appointments column and add to your 'Things to do' list.

Tuesday 3 March

Time	Appointments	Things to do
9.00 am	Daily briefing with rest of team.	Check St Cuthbert's order form
9.30 am		
10.00 am	Phone St Cuthbert's to discuss order	Prepare for Health & safety meeting
10.30 am		
11.00 am		
11.30 am	Meeting with suppliers	
12.00		
12.30 pm		
1.00 pm		
1.30 pm		
2.00 pm	Health & Safety Committee Meeting	
2.30 pm		
3.00 pm	Invoices	
3.30 pm		
4.00 pm	Make sure invoices are in post	
4.30 pm		
5.00 pm	.	
5.30 – 9 pm		

Checkpoint

Compare your appointments and 'Things to do' list with another student's. Have you included everything you need to? If not, add to your diary page. Have you filled in anything incorrectly? If so, cross it out.

English: The Basic Skills

Pair activity

2 You now have to deal with phone messages. The following two messages have been left on your voicemail. In your pair, take it in turns to read the messages aloud. The listener to each message needs to:

- decide on the appropriate action to take
- make a note of this on both diary pages

If the listener needs to hear the message again, he or she should ask the speaker to repeat it.

Voicemail message

Hello, this is the secretary at Perry Bush Primary School in Birmingham. I wonder whether you could call me back about an order we'd like to submit for next term. Before we make the order we just wanted to check if there were price rises in the pipeline. My name is Pam Felixstowe and my number is 0121 745 8888. Could you ring me back sometime between 1.30 and 2 today? Thanks now.

Voicemail message

Erm, sorry to bother you at work. This is Weltham's garage here. Your car's ready to be picked up whenever suits you ... I'm afraid there was a bit of work to do for the MOT but nothing you weren't expecting. We're open till 5.30 ... The total cost is £140 including VAT ... Okay then, bye.

Responding in detail

Some communications require a very careful and detailed response, particularly when a customer is annoyed. At your daily briefing your boss hands you a letter that arrived on his desk the day before. He wants you to deal with it urgently. Read the letter on page 69 carefully before doing activity 3.

3 You are going to decide how best to respond to this letter of complaint.

a The first thing you need to do is identify the three different things the writer is complaining about. Re-read the letter and list the three things.

b The next thing you need to do is identify possible solutions that would make the customer happy. Below are some of the things you could do. Read them carefully and decide which actions are the most appropriate.

- Ring and apologise for difficulties in contact and the late delivery.
- Explain that the company has had problems with its delivery service.
- Make sure the order is sent out on next week's delivery.
- Order a special delivery to be delivered to the school the next day.
- E-mail the writer and apologise for the writer not being able to contact you by phone.
- Tell the writer the old manager was sacked for making promises he couldn't keep.
- Send five complimentary packs of exercise books as an apology for the inconvenience caused.

16 **Organising your day**

Brooklands Primary School, Brooklands Avenue,
Newtown, Essex NT12 4RY

brooklands.newtown@aol.com   09437 622504

Edusupplies4U,
PO Box 144,
London EC4 7FR

27 February

re. Late and damaged exercise books

Dear Sir or Madam,

Having attempted to reach you by phone on three previous occasions without success, I am forced to write.

On 17 February we received fifteen parcels of exercise books from your company (Ref. BPS3254B). This order was five weeks late in arriving, despite the fact that your manager had personally promised that the books would be here for the start of the spring term. When they did arrive, they were in a terrible state. The packaging was ripped and the books were dirty, wet and obviously unusable.

As several of our students are now writing on paper, we need these books as a matter of urgency. As you know, Brooklands Primary has been a good customer of yours for many years. However, if we do not get an early response to this complaint we will be looking elsewhere for a new supplier.

Yours faithfully,

Kim Hodges

Kim Hodges
(School Bursar)

4 Your boss e-mails you later in the day, wanting to know exactly how you have dealt with this problem. Write an e-mail back to him explaining the action you have taken or will be taking, and the reasons for it.

Checkpoint

Show your e-mail to another student, who is playing the part of your boss. He or she should give you feedback on the appropriateness of the action you have taken or will be taking.

Summary

In this unit you have:

- read and listened to a range of messages and taken appropriate action
- responded to each point in a letter of complaint.

17 Safety first

FOR YOUR SAFETY AND COMFORT

SAFETY ON BOARD
Our Crews are specially trained in the safety and security of all passengers and it is an offence to refuse to obey any lawful command of the Captain and Crew, which includes the illumination of passenger signs. Anyone breaking these laws could be refused carriage outward or return by ourselves or any other UK airline and is liable to be subsequently prosecuted under the Air Navigation Act. Our Crew's primary concern is YOUR safety at all times.

SEATBELTS
During take-off and landing seatbelts must be fastened and seats and tables secured in the upright position. You are advised to keep your seatbelt loosely fastened throughout the flight and at any time when requested by the Captain or Crew. Infants travelling on a passenger's lap will require a child safety belt, which our Cabin Crew will be happy to fit for you.

PASSENGER BEHAVIOUR
Jet2.com expect our passengers to behave in a responsible manner and we will not tolerate unacceptable behaviour. This includes foul language and any other behaviour that reduces other passengers' enjoyment of the flight and causes them, or our staff, any degree of distress, discomfort or unnecessary inconvenience. We reserve the right to ban passengers from future flights if their behaviour is a threat to the safety of our passengers and Crew.

HAND LUGGAGE
One piece of hand luggage is allowed per passenger in addition to a handbag or camera, providing its weight is less than 10kg and it is no larger than 46cm x 30cm x 23cm. Excess hand luggage will be placed in the hold. Light or soft articles should be stowed in the overhead luggage compartments, heavier items under seats. Items lying loose on empty seats or obstructing the aisles or emergency exits are dangerous and you will be asked to remove them.

MOBILE PHONES AND ELECTRONIC EQUIPMENT
Once the aircraft is at cruising altitude and the Captain has turned off the 'Fasten Seat Belt' sign, you are free to use laptops, CD players, MP3 players, computer games and most other electronic items. However, for safety reasons, mobile phones (even in 'flight mode') and any other devices with wireless communications e.g. XCA Blackberry handheld, are strictly forbidden at all times while you are on-board. Electronic equipment of any kind is not permitted during taxi, take-off and landing.

COMFORT
Changes in the cabin air pressure may cause some slight discomfort with your ears. You can relieve this by swallowing hard, yawning or holding your nose while gently breathing out with your mouth closed. Flying also causes your body to dehydrate so you are advised to have something to drink that is not alcoholic.

IN-FLIGHT SERVICE
On your flight we will be offering you a comprehensive choice of hot and cold drinks as well as a selection of delicious snacks, including sandwiches and confectionery. Our Cabin Crew will be delighted to offer you a chance to purchase items from our fantastic range of tax paid goods from our Sky Shop, including fragrances, cosmetics, toys and gifts at low prices – take advantage of our great savings against high street prices.

17 **Safety first**

> **In this unit ...**
> you will identify the main points in a text and re-present the information in a different way, as both a spoken and a written piece.

The article on the opposite page is taken from an airline in-flight magazine. It contains important information for the safety and comfort of the airline's passengers.

Reading in detail

Readers sometimes make mistakes because they have not read a text with sufficient care. It is particularly important to read safety instructions closely and to make sure you have properly understood them.

Read the text on page 70 closely. The following multiple-choice questions give you four possible answers. Only one of these is correct. Identify the correct answer to each question.

1 MP3 players:
  a can never be used on board
  b can be used during take-off and landing
  c can be used when the 'Fasten Seat Belt' sign is switched off
  d can be used at cruising altitude when the 'Fasten Seat Belt' sign is switched off.

2 Passengers can relieve ear discomfort by:
  a stretching
  b swallowing hard
  c having a non-alcoholic drink
  d holding their breath.

3 Seatbelts:
  a need only be fastened during take-off and landing
  b must be loosely fastened at all times
  c must be fastened during take-off and landing
  d need not be worn by infants.

4 Passengers who break airline laws:
  a will be thrown off the plane immediately
  b will be asked to return by another UK airline
  c are liable to subsequent prosecution
  d are likely to be arrested at the airport.

5 The Sky Shop:
  a sells duty-free goods
  b sells tax paid goods
  c sells everything at low prices
  d is more expensive than the high street.

6 Hand luggage:
  a must all be stowed in the overhead compartments
  b must be stowed under the seats
  c may be placed on empty seats
  d must be the right size and weigh less than 10kg.

7 Jet2.com expects passengers:
  a to stay seated at all times
  b not to tolerate unacceptable behaviour
  c to behave in a responsible manner
  d to buy snacks and drinks on board.

8 Mobile phones:
  a are strictly forbidden at all times
  b are not permitted during taxi, take-off and landing
  c may be used if 'hands free'
  d may be used if in 'flight mode'.

Checkpoint

Check your answers with another student. Where your answers are different, look back at the text and decide who is correct.

English: The Basic Skills

Formal language

The 'For Your Safety and Comfort' leaflet on page 70 was written for adult passengers. This is evident from the formality of the language that is used. The first column of the table on the right shows two of the formal phrases used in the first paragraph. The second column shows two less formal alternatives.

Formal language	Less formal language
obey any lawful command	do as you are told
could be refused carriage	may not be let to travel

9 Copy and complete the following table by writing in the right-hand column less formal alternatives for the phrases taken from the leaflet.

Formal language	Less formal language
is liable to be subsequently prosecuted	
any degree of distress, discomfort or unnecessary inconvenience	
We reserve the right to	
are strictly forbidden at all times	
Electronic equipment of any kind is not permitted	

Selecting relevant information

The information you include in a text depends on the intended audience. 'For Your Safety and Comfort' was written for adults. You are going to decide which bits of it are most relevant to a younger audience.

Pair activity

10 Work with a partner. You are both responsible for a party of six school children, aged eight to nine years, who are travelling with Jet2.com. Before you board the plane, you are going to give the children a short talk about what they must do and how they should behave. Follow these steps:

Step 1 Together, decide what is relevant to the children and make notes. Leave out anything that is not relevant to the children. For example, after reading the first paragraph your notes might be:

> Notes: must obey Captain/Crew
> cld refuse to take you

Step 2 Think about the order in which you want to give your instructions.

You do not need to follow the order used in 'For Your Safety and Comfort'. Number your notes in your chosen order. Highlight the most important bits as you may want to repeat them for emphasis.

Step 3 Think about the words and the tone of voice you should use when speaking to the children. Look back to your answers to question 9 to get some ideas for less formal language suitable for children.

Step 4 Take it in turns to practise your talk. Give feedback to each other on whether:

- you included all the important points
- the instructions were given clearly in language the children could understand
- your tone of voice was appropriate.

Adapting written instructions

Children often find it useful to have a written reminder of the things they can and can't do. The vocabulary and phrasing should be simple, clear and straightforward. Instructions can be presented in a variety of forms for interest and simplicity. For example, you could:

- create two lists of 'Can do' and 'Can't do'
- use ticks and crosses to reinforce the message
- use pictures or emoticons to reinforce the message.

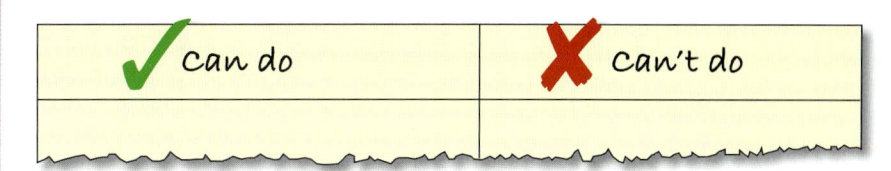

✓ Can do	✗ Can't do

11 a You are going to create a written reminder list for the same children to take on board their flight. Use the notes and talk you gave as a guide for what details to include in your written instructions.

b Before writing the instructions, think about:
- the kind of language you should use
- how to organise the detail
- how to present the detail.

c Aim to produce a clear and interesting instruction sheet that is suitable for young children.

Checkpoint

Work in a group of four. Each of you will need a copy of the table below. Decide who is A, B, C and D.

Assess the instruction sheet of each member of your group, including your own. Your comments should indicate the reason for the score you have given.

When you have assessed all four pieces, show your comments and scores to the other members of your group.

Review your own writing in the light of the comments of the group, and make any changes that you think will improve it.

	Appropriate use of language Comment	Score 1–3	Organisation Comment	Score 1–3	Presentation Comment	Score 1–3	Total
A							
B							
C							
D							

Summary

In this unit you have:
- read a complex text in detail
- identified formal use of language
- selected relevant information
- adapted a text for a different audience.

18 Get to the point

No date – how long has this been lying here?

4 Weir Side
Nanthorpe
Fallowness
FT3 9KT

Dear Sir,

I want to complain. I had to get in touch with my bank about a **mistake** it made.

I rang the number on the web page and waited ages before I got **someone** who couldn't help and **wouldn't** put me on to his manager. He just gave me another number to ring. I waited ages again and then rang off.

I'm really cross about **this**. It costs a lot to phone and I still haven't got an **answer**. I want you to **sort it out** for me soon.

Yours,
K Jones

What was the mistake?
How can I check?
What's the account number?

Who?

I wonder why not?

Is he cross about the phone call or the mistake?

But what is the question?

I would if I knew what he wanted sorting ...

There isn't enough information. I'll have to get some more.

18 **Get to the point**

In this unit ...

you will learn how to write a successful letter of complaint.

Many people write letters of complaint. Some are more successful than others. Read the example of a letter written to a bank manager on page 74.

Problems

The bank manager's thoughts on reading the letter are shown to you opposite.

1 Using the bank manager's annotations to help you, list the different reasons why the first letter of complaint is unlikely to be successful. You should make at least five different points.

Solutions

A formal letter of complaint can be more effective than a phone call. It can provide proof of exactly what had been said and can be used for further action if needed. It's important to make sure a formal letter of complaint is written well in order to get the desired result.

2 Now read the following letter of complaint closely.

> 4 Weir Side
> Nanthorpe
> Fallowness FT3 9KT
>
> 03/05/07
>
> The Manager
> West Land Bank PLC, Fallowness
>
> Re. account: T97563200052
>
> Dear Sir or Madam,
>
> I recently needed to contact my bank about an error on my bank statement. It showed my account as overdrawn but I knew this was not the case.
>
> I rang the number on your web page and spent fifteen minutes waiting to be put through to the right section. When I did get through, the person who took my call, Jason Barr, was unable to answer my query. I asked to be put through to his line manager but he said that was not possible because of company policy. He then gave me another number to ring. I rang this number but, after another ten minutes' wait, I put the phone down.
>
> I feel this is a very bad way for your bank to treat its customers. The phone calls were all at my expense and I still have not had a satisfactory reply to my query. I would be grateful if you would let me know how I can resolve my problem without spending more money.
>
> I look forward to hearing from you within the next ten days.
>
> Yours faithfully,
>
> Mr K. Jones

English: The Basic Skills

Content and language

To write a successful letter of complaint you need to think about both **content** and **language**.

Content: how can I make my complaint clearly and get what I want?
There are four simple steps to follow to get the content right:
- state the problem clearly
- give the relevant details
- make clear what you want done
- give a date by which you want it done.

3 Check that the writer of the second letter covers the four bullet points by identifying where they appear in the letter, for example:
- state the problem clearly – paragraph 1

4 Compare the two letters of complaint. List the details included in the second letter that do not appear in the first. How would these details help the bank manager to sort out the problem?

Language: what kind of language should I use to help me get what I want?
A letter of complaint is almost always formal and requires formal use of language.

5 Look at the following phrases. Letters a–g are more formal ways of expressing the ideas in numbers 1–7. All of a–g are used in the second letter. Copy and complete the table below, matching each number to the appropriate letter.
The first one is done for you.

1	say something to my bank	a	was unable to answer my query
2	he didn't have a clue	b	without incurring further expense
3	your lousy set-up	c	all at my expense
4	he said I couldn't do it	d	your current inefficient system
5	I had to pay for the lot	e	he said that was not possible
6	without it costing me a bomb	f	contact my bank
7	it said I didn't have any money	g	it recorded my account as overdrawn

1	2	3	4	5	6	7
f						

18 **Get to the point**

Writing a letter of complaint

You are now going to write your own formal letter of complaint. Your aim is to write a clear and organised letter using appropriate language.

6 a Choose one of the following situations about which to write a letter of complaint.

You bought a pair of expensive trainers with your birthday money. Within a week the stitching at the front was splitting. You took them back to the shop where you bought them but the assistant refused to exchange them or refund your money. Write a formal letter of complaint to the manager of the shop. Make up your own dates and names for the trainers, the shop and the assistant.

You were given a gift card at Christmas to spend at a particular shop. You put it in a drawer and forgot about it. Six months later you found it and went to spend it. The shop assistant refused to accept it, saying it was out of date. There was no expiry date on the gift card. Write a formal letter of complaint to the manager of the shop. Make up your own dates and names for the shop and the assistant.

b Write your letter. Remember to get the **content** right by:
- stating the problem clearly
- giving the relevant details
- making clear what you want done
- giving a date by which you want it done.

Remember to get the **language** right by:
- using language formally.

Checkpoint

When you have finished, check your letter against the 'Remember to …' bullets and make any useful changes.

Imagine you are the manager of the shop. Explain how you would respond to the letter you have written. Give your reasons.

Summary

In this unit you have:
- identified how to make a complaint clearly in a letter
- compared two letters of complaint
- identified the formal use of language in a letter of complaint
- written a letter of complaint.

19 Virtual writing

In this unit ...
you will learn about using informal and formal language to suit your purpose and audience.

The way we write depends on our purpose and audience. Blogs are a relatively new form of writing (ask your parents!). In some ways a blog is similar to a diary, in that it often gives an account of the day-to-day detail of one person's life. However, whereas most diaries are just intended for the writer to read, a blog has a much wider audience.

Blog style

Blogs are often written in an informal style. The writers aim to give the impression they are talking directly to their readers.

1 Read the following entry, taken from a regularly updated blog. Identify and list:
- **a** the range of punctuation used for effect
- **b** the use of non-standard English or slang
- **c** the range of font styles used for effect.

ANOTHER NIGHT – ANOTHER DOLLAR. WELL KINDA.

Braved Arctic conditions *(cool in shirt sleeves)* and crossed the road to work earlier. There was me thinking that it was just going to be another routine evening at work but OH NO. The sneaky gits had put me on training without telling me **: (** - had to train a new assistant called Danielle *(who I knew by sight)* but I know that she hangs around with a girl called Marcie who is a complete and **utter nutter**!! who everyone hates - naturally I feared the worst. **: (**

How wrong can you be? Danielle was fantastic. I really like her. Turns out she's not a friend of Marcie after all – that's a relief **:)**

Unfortunately I looked a right idiot when I fell over and knocked a whole display shelf over – looked so attractive ... NOT.

---

2 Write the text for your own blog entry. Your audience is likely to be people of your own age. Your purpose is to inform and entertain them so that they will want to come back and read your next instalment.

Checkpoint

In a group of three or four, read and assess your blog entries. Decide how well each one:
- is written in an informal style
- informs the reader
- entertains the reader.

Award a mark out of nine for each blog entry by giving up to three points to each area.

19 **Virtual writing**

Formal style

There are many times when writing in an informal style is not appropriate. Articles published on the Internet are most often written in standard English and use conventional punctuation and font styles. There is usually a wider range of vocabulary, more suited to an older audience.

3
- **a** Read the following article, 'The Teenage Blog Outbreak'. Make a list of the words you would place under the heading: *Vocabulary suited to an older audience*.
- **b** Check the meaning of any words you are unsure of in a dictionary.
- **c** Compare your list with a partner's. After discussion, add or delete any words as appropriate.

The Teenage Blog Outbreak

By Ken Snodin

Blogs are the new buzzword in cyberspace. Anyone and everyone who uses the Internet now knows about the concept of blogging. Though males and females, young and old alike are blogging away, it is the teenagers who have the briskness to use this new virtual platform to its maximum potential.

Having grown up using the computer and the Internet for a large number of their informational needs, these first-generation computer users are at ease when they convey their opinions, thoughts and feelings using the web technology. The use of various platforms of communication on the net comes extremely naturally to them. Unlike older writers who sometimes tend to experience moments of stagnation, the teens can be seen blogging effortlessly.

The rapid emergence of blogs can be attributed to the unequalled characteristic of the platform where teens can acquire a sense of satisfaction from expressing themselves, while remaining anonymous if they want to. Teens create their own blogging space and invite friends, peers and even strangers to join in. This allows them to receive the much-needed attention that many youngsters today want. But, one of the most frightful nightmares of a teen is the fear that a parent or a custodian will chance upon his or her blog.

Though teenagers can write with great alacrity on the blogging platforms, they have very little experience of writing beyond the Internet. This is primarily because publishers of magazines, journals and newspapers are extremely sceptical of publishing young writers. This discourages the youngsters and is probably throttling a major talent which is emerging.

Blogging has found acceptability among the youth since it allows them a forum wherein they can express themselves and showcase their talents without the restraining arms of the publisher. The large reach of this new-age phenomenon grants them the flexibility of using their technical skills to acquire attention and to gain a readership for their writing.

'The Teenage Blog Outbreak' by Ken Snodin, © content-articles.com

Paragraph order

In the article on the previous page the writer is explaining why blogs are popular with teenagers. The ideas are presented in a clear and logical order. This allows the reader to follow the explanation more easily. Paragraphs are used to mark the stages of the explanation.

4 Identify the different stages of the explanation by completing the following sentences which describe the content of each paragraph:

Paragraph 1: introduces the main subject which is about blogs and teenagers' use of them.

Paragraph 2: explains …

Paragraph 3: develops explanation …

Paragraph 4: introduces a new idea about …

Paragraph 5: acts as a conclusion and sums up why …

Write an internet article

Many articles like the one on the previous page appear on the internet. They are written in standard English.

5 You are going to plan and write your own internet article. Your purpose is to explain to adults what MSN® is and why it is popular with teenagers. If you do not know about MSN®, either find out about it or choose a different subject related to the internet.

Follow these stages.

Stage 1 – Content
Jot down the different things you know about MSN®. These might be to do with:
- what MSN® is
- how it works
- things to do
- things not to do
- examples of personal experiences.

Stage 2 – Plan
Decide on a clear and logical order in which to present your explanation. It will help you to plan the content of your paragraphs. Aim to plan four or five paragraphs. Decide how you will develop the main ideas in each paragraph.

Stage 3 – Style
Think about your style of writing. You should aim to write in a formal style and to use a wide vocabulary range.

Stage 4 – Draft
Write the first draft of your article. Read through every paragraph to check you have followed your plan and expressed your ideas clearly, before moving on to the next one.

19 Virtual writing

Checkpoint

In the same group as before, read and assess your articles. Decide how well each one:

- has ordered the ideas clearly and logically
- has used detail to develop the explanation
- has used a formal style and an adult vocabulary.

Award a mark out of nine for each article by giving up to three points to each area.

Summary

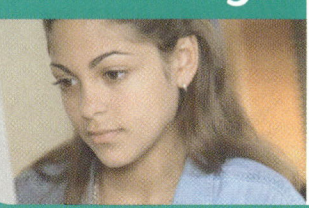

In this unit you have:

- examined the informal style of blogs
- written your own blog entry
- examined the vocabulary and paragraph structure of a formal article
- written your own internet article.

20 Face to face

In this unit ...
you will think about the impact you have on others and how to use body language and pace of speech to get the results you want.

Read on to find out about the importance of body language when speaking and listening.

Body language

Did you know ... ?

The first 30 seconds to two minutes usually make or break the connection between two people when they meet for the first time.

Many interviews are unsuccessful, not because of what is said but because of non-verbal behaviour such as eye contact, posture, facial expression and gestures.

It is important to be aware of your body language and in control of the impression you create.

1 Look at the photographs. For each one, describe the body language and say what impression it creates.

A   B   C   D   E   F

Pair activity

2 Work with a partner and take it in turns to create poses to suit the following situations. Help your partner by suggesting how they could improve each pose.

Sitting – appearing interested in the conversation.
Sitting – appearing bored by the conversation.
Standing – meeting someone for the first time who you want to impress.
Standing – not listening closely to someone who is talking to you.

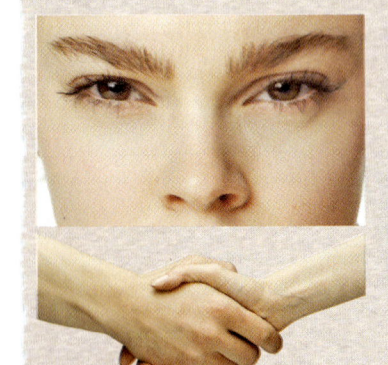

3 a Only a mirror or another person can tell us things about our appearance. With a partner, take it in turns to practise the following aspects of body language. Give feedback to each other on the impression that is given.

eye contact	crossing arms	a weak handshake	smiling
fidgeting	lack of eye contact	good posture	biting nails
yawning	slouching	a firm handshake	frowning

b Agree the three things from the above list which you think are most likely to make a good impression in an interview and why.

20 **Face to face**

Pace and pausing

Body language is important, but how you speak also affects the impression you make.

Effective speakers:
- control the pace at which they speak
- pause for effect.

To be an effective speaker you need to develop these skills. This takes practice.

4 Practise reading the following news item aloud.
- Start by reading the item silently to familiarise yourself with the words and content.
- Then, think about the pace at which you should read it – too quickly and your listeners cannot follow it; too slowly and they get bored.
- Finally, think about where you should pause for effect – the punctuation may help you decide.

© Michael Perham

> Yesterday, Michael Perham, a 14-year-old schoolboy from Hertfordshire, became the youngest person ever to cross the Atlantic singlehanded.
>
> Michael was escorted into the calm waters of English Harbour in Antigua by a flotilla of small boats. Immaculately turned out in white T-shirt and white cap, he punched the air and a steel band struck up a jaunty tune as he tied up.
>
> Setting foot on dry land for the first time in more than six weeks, he said it felt "absolutely fantastic". He hugged his father, Peter, who arrived a few minutes later having shadowed his son across the Atlantic in another yacht, always staying a mile or so away.
>
> Michael, who has sailed since he was seven, came up with the idea of the voyage after watching footage of the previous youngest solo transatlantic sailor – Sebastian Clover, 15, from the Isle of Wight. He now has ambitions of sailing around the world but, for the moment, will have to concentrate once more on his GCSEs.

Extract adapted from 'You did it, son', Steven Morris, The Guardian*, 4 January 2007*

Checkpoint

Work in pairs. Take it in turns to be a newsreader on TV and to read the above article using appropriate body language, pace and pausing.

Decide who is the more effective newsreader. Give reasons for your decision.

83

English: The Basic Skills

FORTUNE MILLION POUND GIVEAWAY

A First you need to think about your purpose and audience. You want to convince five millionaires to give you some of their money. Jot down ideas about:
- what kinds of thing might interest them
- what kinds of thing would definitely not interest them
- what you would need to do to convince them.

B Now you need to choose your subject. It could be one of the following or something else:
- a club or sports association that needs money to keep going
- something that is desperately needed to improve the quality of life in your area
- a charity in which you have a particular interest
- a new product or invention that needs cash input.

Make notes on what you could say about your chosen subject.

C Decide on which details to select for your presentation. Aim to select the details most likely to gain the millionaires' support.

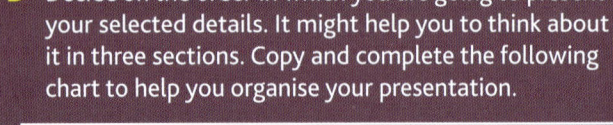

D Decide on the order in which you are going to present your selected details. It might help you to think about it in three sections. Copy and complete the following chart to help you organise your presentation.

Section 1: *your introduction*
Aim to get them interested right from the start. Make it clear what you are going to be talking about.

Section 2: *the main body of your presentation*
Include the details that are most likely to interest the millionaires, for example why the money is needed, how much is needed (don't be greedy), the difference the money would make, the reasons for your personal interest in this subject.

Section 3: *your conclusion*
Aim to reinforce the points you have made and maybe add one new one. Make it clear when you have finished with a final appeal to the millionaires.

Making a presentation

Have you seen the TV programme *Fortune: Million Pound Giveaway*?

In this programme, five millionaires attempt to give away £1m of their own money to those members of the public who can convince them that they deserve a share.

Group activity

5 Work in groups of three or four. Your task is to make a successful presentation to try to win a share of £1m. You will have three minutes in which to make your presentation. To make every minute count, you need to prepare carefully. Follow stages A to H listed above.

20 **Face to face**

E Together, write a script for your presentation. You need to do this so you can time it and make sure you make full use of the allowed three minutes and do not run over time.

F Allocate different parts of the presentation to members of the group and decide whether you will learn your speech or use a prompt card. You must not simply read your speech as you need to maintain eye contact with the millionaires. You could use a simple prompt card like this:

> **Prompt list**
> - Intro: chosen subject
> - why money needed –
> - how much needed –
> - difference it would make –
>   reasons/personal
> - extra point and final appeal

G Remind yourselves of the importance of appropriate body language. Picture yourselves giving your presentation. What body language will you use?

H Think about the pace of your presentation. Remember it should not be too fast or too slow. Decide where you should pause for extra effect.

© Fever Media

Checkpoint

Those listening to the presentation should award a score out of ten to each group on the basis of:

- clear presentation
- appropriate body language
- effective pace and pausing.

The group with the highest marks has given the most effective presentation.

Summary

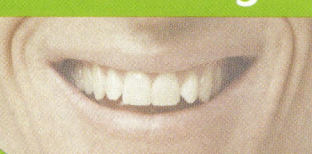

In this unit you have:

- learned how body language affects an audience
- learned the importance of pace and pausing in speech
- prepared and given a group presentation.

21 Presentation matters

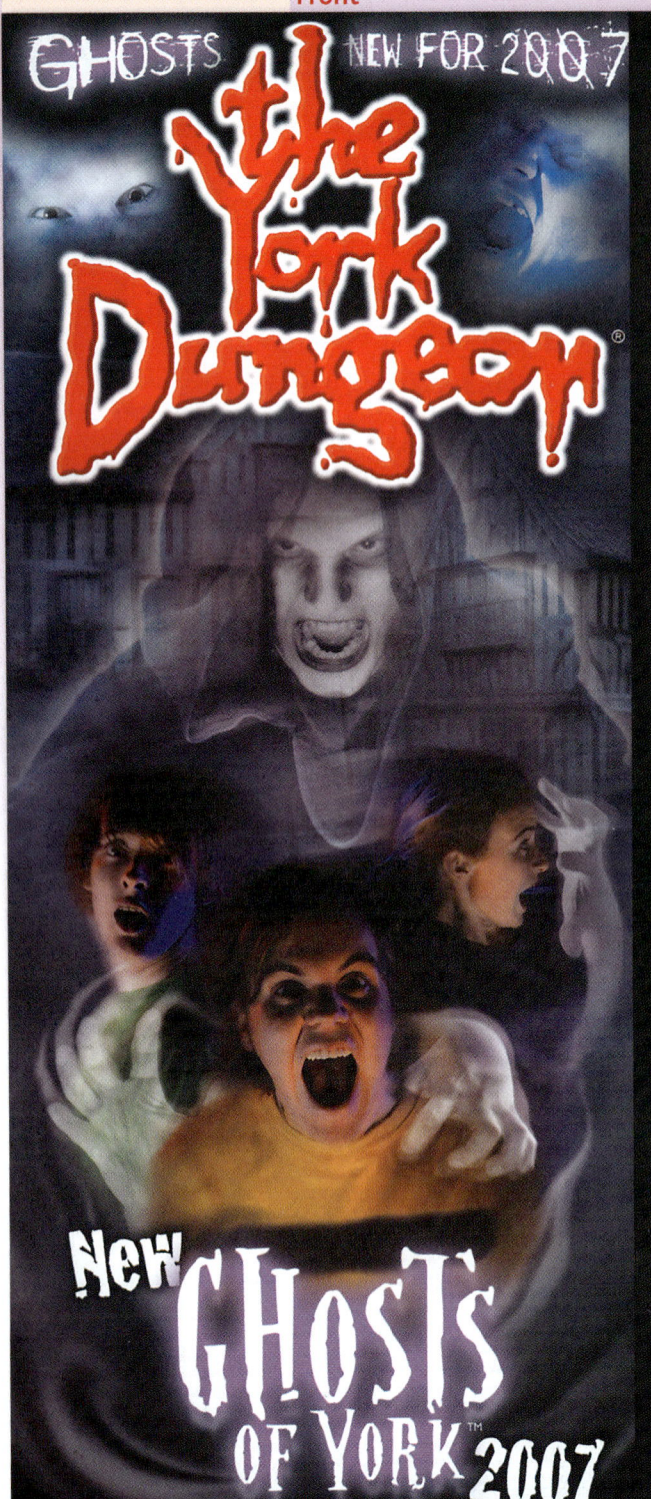

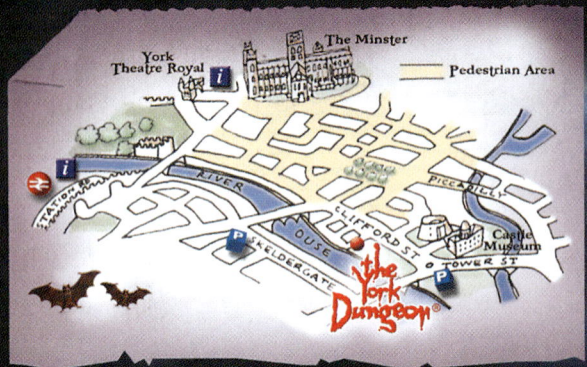

Front

GHOSTS NEW FOR 2007
the York Dungeon
New GHOSTS OF YORK 2007

Back

12 Clifford Street, York Y01 9RD

Railway station: 10 minutes walk from York Station in Station Road.
Buses: 5 minutes walk from Bus Station, Rougier Street.
Parking: Cars - St. George's Field and Castle Car Parks.
Coaches - Kent Street, Union Terrace.

~ *Groups, Schools and Private Events* ~

The Dungeon is great for gruesome group and school bookings and for private events. Call 01904 632599 or email york.dungeons@merlinentertainments.biz

Open seven days a week excluding Christmas Day.
April – Sept: 10:30am to 5:00pm.
Easter, Whitsun & Summer holidays: 10am to 5:30pm.
Nov – Jan: 11:00am to 4:00pm.
Oct, Feb & March: 10:30am to 4:30pm.
Opening hours subject to change. Closing times stated are last admissions.
Please check www.thedungeons.com for up to date information.

The Dungeon is not recommended for those of a nervous disposition or young children. Children under 15 must be accompanied by an adult.

Visitors are reminded that for technical, operational and other reasons, any of the attractions or facilities indicated may be altered, closed, removed or otherwise unavailable at any time.

~ *Fast Track Tickets* ~

Book online and benefit from our best price guarantee fast track tickets! Ideal for weekends, bank holidays and during the school holidays.

www.thedungeons.com

Merlin Entertainments (Dungeons) Limited
Registered office: 3 Market Close, Poole, Dorset BH15 1NQ
Registered Number: 3671067

© Merlin Entertainments

21 Presentation matters

In this unit …
you will examine how the presentation and layout of a text contribute to its effectiveness.

Writers and designers often work together to achieve maximum impact on the reader. Look at and read the *front* page of the leaflet for York Dungeon on the opposite page.

Thinking about presentation

Designers use a range of presentational features. These include colours, fonts, graphics and illustrations. They also need to decide where these features should appear on a page.

Group activity

1. Look at the front page of the leaflet. In groups of two or three, jot down any points you can make about:
   - the size and colour of the text
   - the illustrations
   - the ways the different colours are used
   - the layout or organisation of the detail.

2. Share your ideas with another group. Add anything to your list that you had not thought of.

Interpreting presentation

When looking at features of presentation it is important to:
- examine them closely
- use what you already know to help you interpret them
- think about the effect they will have on the reader.

Read the two comments on the right about the presentation of the title of the leaflet. The first student simply states what he sees. The second student uses what he knows to comment on the effect of the colour and to work out why that colour has been used.

> The front page has the name "the York Dungeon" written in large red font surrounded by white to make it stand out.

> The font used for "the York Dungeon" has a Gothic effect which reminds the reader of olden times. It is written in red to make you think of danger and blood. It's made to look as though the blood is still dripping to give a scary effect and to give the impression that this is a frightening place to visit.

3. **a** Read the student's comment below about the illustrations and words on the front of the leaflet.

   > There is a picture of a ghost on the front page with three frightened young people. The children are all screaming. They make the place look scary. The word 'new' is repeated to make it stand out.

   b Develop and write a more detailed comment. Before writing your comment, think about:
   - the number of ghosts
   - why the children are looking in different directions
   - the expressions on the faces of the children and the ghosts
   - anything the main ghost reminds you of
   - why the word *new* is repeated
   - the intended effects of the words and the illustrations on the reader.

English: The Basic Skills

How information is presented

More detailed information can also be presented visually. The presentation needs to be appropriate and appealing, and also clear and easy to follow.

4 Look at and read the *back* page of the leaflet on page 86.
  a Describe how the information is organised on this page.
  b Why do you think similar colours are used on the back cover as on the front?
  c Study the map and the information immediately below it. How helpful is the map? Give reasons for your answer.
  d Give possible reasons why you are not told the price of entrance to the dungeons.
  e Explain why you are given the website address.
  f Why do you think the picture of the woman appears on this page?

Checkpoint

Compare your answers to question 4 with another student's. Where you have different answers, talk about the reasons for this.

Identifying purpose and audience

The **purpose** of a text is the reason why it was written.

The **audience** of a text is the intended reader.

Texts often have more than one purpose and audience.

5 Copy and complete the headings below.
  a Start by identifying the intended purposes and audiences of the front and back pages of the York Dungeon leaflet.
  b Then give your reasons for your answer.
  c Why do you think front and back pages of leaflets often have different purposes and audiences?

Front page
Purpose(s)
Audience(s)
Reasons for thinking this

Back page
Purpose(s)
Audience(s)
Reasons for thinking this

21 Presentation matters

Comparing texts

When you compare texts you find the similarities and differences between them.

6 Make your own notes on the similarities and differences between the front and back pages of the York Dungeon leaflet. When doing so, think about the following:
- your first impressions of each page
- what is on each page
- how colour is used
- the images used
- the intended purposes
- the intended audiences.

7 Copy the following sentences which compare the front and back pages of the leaflet. Make the correct choice from the phrase bank below to complete each of the sentences.

> The front page of the York Dungeon leaflet contains images of three ghosts and three children whereas the back page _____.
>
> On the front page the name of the place is written in _____ and it looks as though the blood is dripping from it. The same place name is repeated on the map on the back page but it is _____.
>
> The ghostly images and the repetition of the word _____ on the front page give the impression that this is a scary place. Although there are no ghostly images on the back cover there is a picture of a spooky woman, which is _____.

| large blood-red font | 'ghosts' | much smaller and has less impact |
| contains information and directions | | also intended to scare |

8 Use your answers to Questions 6 and 7 to help you write three more points of comparison.

Checkpoint

Look back through the unit to help you complete these sentences correctly.

The purpose of a text is …

The audience of a text is …

When you compare texts you …

Summary

In this unit you have:
- examined features of presentation closely
- identified intended purposes and audiences
- compared the front and back pages of a leaflet.

22 Building reports

Stone me! Masons in prize swoop

by *Haydn Lewis* Education Reporter

Two York-trained stonemasons are carving out a career after scooping the top award in their industry.

The Worshipful Company of Masons – one of the oldest Livery Companies in the City of London – has given two young stonemasons, trained at York College, its most prestigious award.

The accolade is named after the Duke of Gloucester and aims to encourage high standards of stonemasonry among young craftsmen.

Piers Merry and Gary Collier have both gained the award after being trained at the college.

Piers qualified at York College in 2003 and now works with master mason Matthias Garn at Bugthorpe, in East Yorkshire. After qualifying, Piers spent three years at the studios of Nathan Hunt, in California, honing his architectural carving skills.

It is for these skills that Piers has received his award.

The judges said that Piers 'has a real passion for what he does … has good hand and eye co-ordination … and is a natural and intuitive carver'.

Gary also qualified from York College in 2003. He was born in Oldham and works for Lloyd & Smith, a firm based in the Lancashire town. He now lives in Slaithwaite. Gary also achieved the Silver Medal at the 2005 WorldSkills in Helsinki and the 2002 Skillbuild.

The judges described Gary as 'a credit to the craft of stone-masonry … a perfectionist who earns the respect of all those he works with …' These awards were presented for the first time in 2007 and will be awarded every two years in future.

The Awards are made to qualified stonemasons in England who, after achieving their qualification in stonemasonry, have worked for a period of five years developing their craft and have demonstrated in their everyday work a high degree of skill in stonemasonry, of carving of stone and considerable improvement since qualifying.

Stonemason at work

© *The Press* Thursday, 11/10/07

22 Building reports

> **In this unit ...**
> you will learn more about how to organise reports and will write two reports of your own, in appropriate language. You will also learn how to use the passive and active voices.

Read the article on page 90. It is an example of a newspaper report. The annotations show you how the report is structured.

Newspaper reports

A newspaper report provides information for readers. It tells the story of something that has happened. Newspaper reports are very varied. They can be about very serious issues such as accidents or wars, or light-hearted matters such as the latest celebrity scandal. Newspaper reports are written with a distinctive structure. This is shown by the annotations and is explained in more detail below.

Lead

This refers to the first paragraph or two, which sum up the main facts of a story. The lead helps readers to decide whether they want to read the full report or turn to the next article. The lead usually addresses questions such as: Who? What? Where? When? How?

1 Read the first two paragraphs of the report on page 90 (the lead) and answer these questions:
 a **Who** is the article about?
 b **Where** are they from?
 c **What** has happened?

Body

This refers to the remaining paragraphs. The body gives more details but they are less important details and it usually includes some relevant quotations. The paragraphs are usually short and the sentences are often simple and direct. Both these features make the report quick and easy to read.

2 Read the body of the report on page 90 and answer these questions to identify some of the extra detail:
 a What are the names of the two stonemasons?
 b Where does Piers now work?
 c Why did Piers receive the award?
 d Where does Gary now work?
 e Why did Gary receive the award?
 f Where were the two stonemasons trained?
 g When were the awards first presented?
 h Which people are quoted in the report?

Pictures and captions

Photographs (and other illustrations and graphics) add interest to the story and help the reader to visualise what is happening. Captions are used to explain them.

3 What does the photograph show you?

Headline and byline

The headline gives some clues to a story's subject. It is designed to attract the readers' attention and may use a play on words to amuse or shock the reader. The headline is often the last thing to be written in the report. The byline usually gives the name of the reporter.

4 Now that you have read the full report, think carefully about the headline. The phrases 'Stone me' and 'Stone the crows' are both informal expressions of surprise. How does the headline play on these?

Write your own newspaper report

Think about a subject for a report you could write for a local newspaper. It could be about a real or imagined incident. For example:

- a group that has raised money for charity
- new facilities in the area, such as a leisure centre
- a sports event or victory
- an annual event such as a festival
- something else of your own choice.

5 You are now going to write your newspaper report on the subject you have chosen. Follow the steps below and what you have learned so far in this unit to help you.

A Once you have chosen your subject, you need to build up details. Use the questions **Who? What? When? Where? Why?** and **How?** to help you make notes. For your report, you can make up details such as names and places and the things that people say.

B Decide on what you will put in your lead, the first one or two paragraphs. Remember, your lead needs to sum up the story for the reader.

C Decide on the order of detail to follow the lead.

D Write your article.

E Now decide on a headline that gives a clue as to what the story is about. You might decide to shock or amuse your reader. Write your headline and byline.

Checkpoint

Read through what you have written and check that:
- you have answered the main questions your reader might have
- your report is organised and clear.

Decide on a suitable photograph that could accompany your report. Write:
- a short description of the photograph you would choose
- the caption you would use for your photograph.

Title: An investigation into whether light is necessary for photosynthesis

Aim *Summary of the investigation*	To measure the amount of starch in leaves under two different conditions, one with light and one without light.	
Apparatus *Details of what is needed to carry out the investigation*	Heatproof mat 2 Boiling tubes Bunsen burner 2 White tiles Tripod Boiling tube rack Gauze Boiling tube holder Enamel mug Permanent felt-tip pen Forceps Reagents: Matches Alcohol, iodine solution	Labels: Beaker, Water, Alcohol, Boiling tube, Leaf, Wire gauze, Tripod, Bunsen burner
Method *Details relating to preparation for the investigation and other relevant issues*	Two geranium plants were destarched, by keeping them in the dark for 48 hours before the experiment started. One plant was placed in the light for 24 hours (plant A) and the other was placed in the dark for 24 hours (plant B). **Safety** Alcohol is flammable and should be kept away from a naked Bunsen burner flame. Safety glasses and a lab coat must be worn and hair must be tied back. If iodine solution is spilt on the skin it must be rinsed off immediately under running tap water to avoid staining. Other normal laboratory rules must be adhered to.	
Procedure *A description of the investigation*	The mug was half-filled with water and placed on the wire gauze on top of the tripod. The Bunsen burner was lit, making sure that the airhole was closed. After opening the airhole, to get a blue flame, the Bunsen burner was placed under the tripod to heat the water. One boiling tube and one tile were labelled 'light' and the other boiling tube and tile were labelled 'dark'. A leaf was then removed from plant A, using the forceps, and placed on the 'light' tile. A leaf was then removed from plant B, using the forceps, and placed on the 'dark' tile. When the water was boiling the leaves were dropped into it, one at a time, for 10 seconds to stop metabolic activities and soften their cuticles. The leaves were removed, using the forceps, and placed into their labelled boiling tubes …	
Results *What the investigation revealed*	The leaf from plant A turned blue-black, and the leaf from plant B stayed brown (iodine solution colour).	
Conclusion *What the results indicate*	As the leaf from plant A turned blue-black when iodine was added, this indicates it had starch in it. As the leaf from plant B stayed brown, this indicates it did not have starch in it. This shows that light is necessary for photosynthesis, as plants are unable to make glucose and then starch without it.	

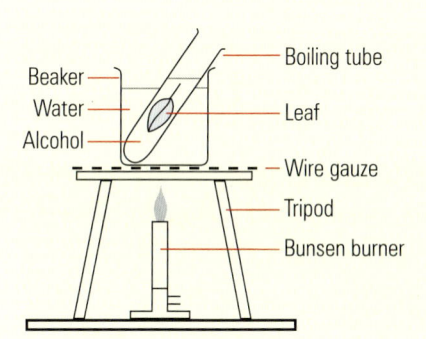

Science report © Deirdre Keating

English: The Basic Skills

The structure of an investigative report

Look at the investigative report on page 93. An investigative report describes a process or gives details of research undertaken. It then draws conclusions based on what has been discovered.

Investigative reports are usually written in the past tense and have a distinctive structure as shown by the annotations.

6 Use the annotations on page 93 to help you answer the following:
  a Place the following in the order they appear in an investigative report.
     Procedure   Title   Apparatus   Conclusion   Aim   Results   Method
  b In your own words, explain the difference between the 'Method' and the 'Procedure'.
  c In your own words, explain the link between the 'Results' and the 'Conclusion'.

The passive voice in investigative reports

Many verbs can be active or passive.

When the verb is active, the subject performs the action, for example:

This is called the active voice.

When the verb is passive, the subject is on the receiving end of the action, for example:

This is called the passive voice.

The passive voice is frequently used in investigative reports to create a more formal tone.

ACTIVE

subject   verb

I placed one plant in the light for 24 hours.

PASSIVE

subject   verb

One plant was placed in the light for 24 hours.

7 Look back at the 'Method' and 'Safety' sections of the investigative report on page 93. Identify and write down the passive voice for the following:
  a I destarched two geranium plants.
  b Wear a lab coat.

8 Copy this table. Sort the sentences that follow it into active and passive. Highlight the subject and the verb in each sentence, as shown in the example:

ACTIVE VOICE	PASSIVE VOICE
subject verb	subject verb
I removed the leaves.	The leaves were dropped into it.

  a I placed the Bunsen burner under the tripod.
  b I labelled one boiling tube and one tile 'light'.
  c A leaf was then removed from plant A.
  d The Bunsen burner was switched off.
  e I poured alcohol into each tube.
  f The leaves were covered.

22 Building reports

Language in investigative reports

Investigative reports of the kind on page 93 are written in clear and precise language. Work out why by doing the following task.

9 Compare each of the following pairs of sentences. In each pair the first sentence is taken from the investigative report on page 93.

A The mug was half-filled with water and placed on the wire gauze on top of the tripod.

B The bright blue birthday mug was only half filled with water. It was placed lovingly on the polished wire gauze, which sat neatly on top of the brand new tripod.

A A leaf was then removed from plant B, using the forceps, and placed on the 'dark' tile.

B A solitary leaf was tenderly removed, with the gentle use of forceps, from plant B and placed with equal care on the dingy dark tile.

a In what ways are the sentences in each pair:
- similar
- different.

b After comparing the pairs of sentences, give two reasons to explain why clear and precise language is the appropriate choice for an investigative report.

Writing your own investigative report

It is important when writing an investigative report to:
- use the passive tense
- keep the language clear and precise
- write in the past tense when describing the procedure.

10 The following paragraph was written by a student who was carrying out an investigation on osmosis. She forgot the rules given on the left. Rewrite the paragraph. Check you have followed each of the rules.

> I got a nice big measuring cylinder and poured 30 cl of distilled water into it. I then took a piece of visking tubing and wet it and tied a knot in one end. After that I filled it with some sucrose solution. Then I tie a knot in the top end with a little bit of thread. I gave it a wash under the tap and then made sure I put in the measuring cylinder carefully and then I start the stop watch. 40 minutes later it was all done so I take the visking bag out of the cylinder and then I looked to see how much water was left in the cylinder and then I measured it.

Summary

In this unit you have:
- learned about the structure of a newspaper report and an investigative report
- written a newspaper report
- learned about appropriate uses of language in formal reports
- rewritten a report using appropriate language.

23 Communicating persuasively

In this unit ...
you will examine the skills needed to communicate information, ideas and opinions effectively and persuasively. You will also practise writing persuasively.

A main part of an advertiser's job is to persuade the reader to buy into the product, whether it is a holiday, a computer product or a clothes store. The advertiser needs to show the product in a positive light and use language to persuade the reader that this is something that should not be missed.

Going on holiday?

When creating an advert for a holiday, the writer starts with a number of basic details about the place. The task is to make the place seem as appealing as possible so that people will want to go there. In the following example of persuasive writing, the advertiser started off with the basic details shown on the right.

> **Notes for the West of Ireland ad**
> Place
> West of Ireland
> Places to visit
> The Burren (limestone region noted for flowers)
> The Slieve League cliffs (highest in Europe)
> Dun Aengus Fort on Aran Islands (2,000 years old)
> St Patrick's mountain (legend: St Patrick rang a bell to rid Ireland of snakes)
> Beaches on the Atlantic coast

1 a Now read what the writer did with these details. The annotations in the first half of the text give clues to help you identify how the writer uses words to persuade the reader.

▮ do these things   ▮ associated with money – you will be better off

Discover a wealth of breathtaking places and have a richer experience in the west of Ireland

Take a car around the west of Ireland and explore the length and breadth of wild, imposing landscapes that will startle and captivate.

The Burren's here, a vast limestone plateau of exotic flowers. There's also the Slieve League cliffs, the highest (and most dramatic) in Europe and 2,000-year-old Dun Aengus Fort on the Aran islands. Discover St Patrick's holy mountain (where he rang the bell that drove the snakes from Ireland) and an endless variety of secluded, deserted beaches, exquisitely carved by the teeming waters of the Atlantic.

It's all here, waiting to be discovered and enjoyed!

▮ something extraordinary   ▮ beautiful and rare   ▮ nothing better

b Now write your own annotations to show what the writer of the advertisement is suggesting by the use of each of the following:

- endless variety
- secluded, deserted beaches
- exquisitely carved
- teeming waters
- waiting

23 Communicating persuasively

Being creative with words

A plain sentence can be transformed by the creative use of words.

2 a Read the following examples. The sentences on the right give the same information as those on the left, but in a more creative way. Look for the words that have been used to make the sentences more interesting.

This street is full of old buildings.	This fascinating street winds on into the distance, packed with imposing, historic buildings that cause the first-time visitor to stand and gaze in awe.
There is a park with a lake and swans on the edge of the town.	Just a few minutes' walk from the busy town centre, you'll discover the peace and tranquillity of Townsend Park. Rest for a while by the lake and watch the swans glide gently across the glistening waters.

b Try being creative with words. Aim to transform the following sentences.

There is a long beach with cliffs on the north side.

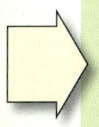

The railway station is big, old and busy.

Writing your own advert

As you have seen, writers can transform basic details by being creative with words. In advertising, they do this to persuade their readers to buy into a product.

3 Choose a place you know well. It doesn't have to be a holiday place – it could be where you live. You are going to write about it in a way that will persuade people to go there. Use the advert for Ireland as a model for your writing. Follow these steps:

A   List four to six details you will include.
B   Place the details in the order in which you will write about them.
C   Add a bit of information about each detail.
D   Think about how you could use words creatively to persuade the reader. Write the words next to the details.
E   Jot down ideas for how you could start and end your writing.
F   Write your persuasive piece. Aim to write between 100 and 150 words.

Checkpoint

Highlight the words in your writing that you have chosen to persuade your reader.

Annotate your writing to show what you think the underlined words suggest.

You should have underlined and annotated at least five examples. If you have not, add more persuasive language to your writing.

English: The Basic Skills

Buying a gadget?

Advertisers are constantly trying to sell us new products. They work in a very competitive world. Sometimes they need to convince an audience, that knows little about the product, that they would benefit from it.

4 a Read the following advert and the annotations.

- read on, this is for you
- directly addresses reader – says again, this is for you
- pattern of three for effect
- it's quick and simple
- reinforces idea that it is simple

PhotoPlus 7

Digital imaging power for everyone!

PhotoPlus 7 is the truly indispensable tool that lets you create, edit and enhance photos and bitmap images in an instant. This sensational, easy-to-use application is ideal for use with your digital camera and scanner and lets everyone go beyond the capabilities of basic digital-imaging software. Combining the award-winning qualities of earlier versions with state-of-the-art digital-imaging technology, the sensational PhotoPlus 7 reaches levels of power and usability previously reserved for users of expensive high-end packages!

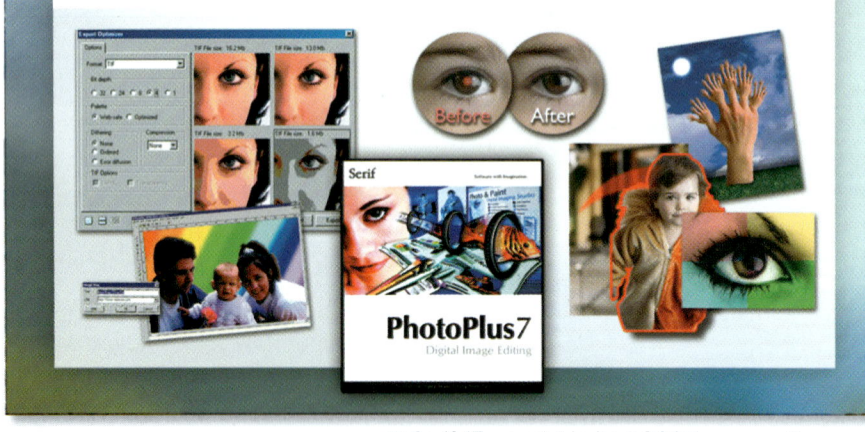

© Serif (Europe) Limited 2007 www.serif.com

b Now write your own annotations to show what the writer of the advert is suggesting by the use of each of the following:

- ideal for use with your digital camera
- lets everyone go beyond
- award-winning qualities
- state-of-the-art
- previously reserved for users of expensive high-end packages!

23 Communicating persuasively

Writing your own

As you have seen, writers sometimes target readers who know very little about the product. They are clever in their use of words, making the reader believe that this product really is for them and that they cannot do without it.

5 Choose a gadget that you know something about. It could be a mobile phone, MP3 player, item of computer software or something completely different. Your aim is to persuade readers who know little about this gadget that they would benefit from it. Follow these steps:

- **A** List three to five details you will include.
- **B** Place the details in the order in which you will write about them.
- **C** Add a bit of information about each detail.
- **D** Next to the details jot down words you could use to persuade the reader.
- **E** Think of how you could start and end your writing.
- **F** Write your persuasive piece. Aim to write between 70 and 100 words.

Checkpoint

Swap your work with a partner. Annotate the words in your partner's writing that you think have been chosen to persuade the readers.

Once you have annotated the writing, award a mark between one and five (where five is the highest) to show how successful they have been in using language persuasively.

English: The Basic Skills

Looking for clothes?

Products and companies often change their image over time and may want to persuade you that the change is for the good. To do this they need to change the way you think about the product or company.

6 a Read the following magazine article closely. The writer of the article aims to persuade the reader that the store has changed by describing how it used to be in the first paragraph and how it is now in the second paragraph.

AS THE AUTUMN STOCK GRADUALLY TAKES UP RESIDENCE IN STORES, there will be one whose clothes you won't recognise. It is a shop you've been studiously ignoring for a few years; one that *used* to do consistently fabulous knitwear, cute skirts and great accessories, but had become a little out of touch. We're talking about Jigsaw, the 35-year-old business that has been looking more like 65.

However, if you head to Jigsaw now prepare for some serious shopping. Because – from its dinky ballerina pumps in purple and its elegant cashmere knits, to perfectly cut wide-leg trousers and a skinny black jumper dress that would give the Olsens a run for their money – the new look Jigsaw has got all the fashion essentials of the season covered. Not the cutting-edge must haves, but the things you will want to wear day in, day out – and to say *Grazia* has gone mad for them is an understatement.

© Words by Melanie Rickey/GRAZIA

  b Which three phrases in the first paragraph suggest the store was behind the times?
  c Choose three phrases from the second paragraph which are used to persuade the reader that the store has changed.

7 The writer details the kind of clothes that are now in store using language to persuade.
  a What adjectives does she use to describe the pumps, the cashmere knits and the wide-leg trousers?
  b What image of the clothes is she trying to create in order to persuade the reader to shop at the store?

23 **Communicating persuasively**

Writing your own

As you have seen, writers sometimes want to change the way you think about a product or a company. They might do this by comparing the past with the present and by using language persuasively.

8 Choose something that you think needs a new image. It could be a sportswear range, a fashion store, a car, a chocolate bar, a magazine or something completely different. Read the following directions before starting to write:

> A You should write two paragraphs.
> B Your first paragraph should show what was wrong with the old image.
> C Your second paragraph should present a persuasive picture of the new image.
> D You should use language to persuade your reader that the product is now worth buying.
> E You should write between 150 and 200 words.

Checkpoint

Read back through the unit and the persuasive pieces you have written.

List five things that you think are important to remember when writing to persuade.

Compare your list with another student's and add any useful points you may have missed.

Summary

In this unit you have:
- examined the techniques writers use to write persuasively
- experimented with transforming plain sentences through the creative use of persuasive language
- written three different persuasive pieces.

24 Complex and clear

In this unit ...
you will examine the skills needed to communicate complex information clearly and effectively. You will also write an informative piece on a complex subject.

A main part of a journalist's job is to give information to the readers. This information may be quite complex and include a number of facts and figures. The journalist's task is to present this complex information in a clear and interesting way.

Organisation of complex information

When presenting complex information the writer needs to avoid bombarding the reader with lots of facts and figures. The information needs to be organised and presented carefully so that key facts and figures are introduced gradually, giving the readers time to absorb them.

1 Read the article below carefully. Then answer the questions that follow to help you examine how the writer of the article organises the information.

Britons tune, click and plug into digital age

In a world of digital TV, video-on-demand and the iPod, radio risked being left behind. There is something rather old-fashioned about switching on your 'wireless', a term more likely to refer to broadband internet these days.

But the latest audience figures published yesterday reveal that we are more in love with the radio than ever before. It is just that we are not listening to it in quite the same way as we used to.

Having seen off the rise of television music channels such as MTV in the 1980s, radio is now piggy backing on the digital revolution, with nearly 12 million people – 26% of the adult population – tuning in via digital radio, digital TV and the internet.

Around 4.4 million listen on their mobile phone, up more than 25% on last year, with 1.8 million of them aged between 15 and 24. 'In this multiplatform environment it's absolutely vital for radio stations to make content ... accessible on as many platforms as possible,' said Paul Jackson, chief executive of Virgin Radio, which became the first to launch on 3G mobile phones in 2005.

Another 2.7 million of us listen to podcasts downloaded on to our iPod or other MP3 player, up from 1.9 million. It is radio, but not as we once knew it.

Extract from 'Radio days are here again as Britons tune, click and plug into digital age', The Guardian, 17/08/07, John Plunkett

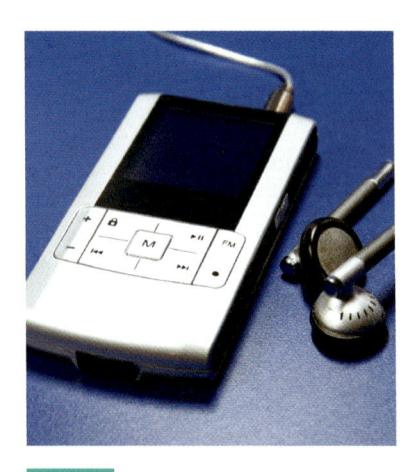

a The writer introduces the subject with his personal opinions. What opinions does he give in the opening paragraph?
b What is the effect of opening the second paragraph with the word 'But'?
c Before presenting the reader with the figures the writer presents conclusions. What two conclusions are given in the second paragraph?
d Suggest reasons why the writer also presents this figure as a percentage of the whole population.
e In the fourth paragraph, how does the writer show the previous year's figure for those who listened to the radio using mobile phones?

24 Complex and clear

    f What additional statistics are used in the fourth paragraph?
    g How does the quotation in paragraph four reinforce what has been said so far?
    h What is the effect of starting the final paragraph with the word "Another"?
    i What is the effect of the final sentence?

Use of complex sentences

The writer of the article on page 102 is writing for an adult audience. He uses a range of sentence structures in the article, including complex sentences. Complex sentences have a main clause and one or more subordinate clauses. A main clause makes complete sense on its own. A subordinate clause does not. The example on the right shows this.

There is something rather old-fashioned about switching on your "wireless", a term more likely to refer to broadband internet these days.

main clause – makes complete sense on its own

subordinate clause – you need to know what the "term" is to make complete sense of it

2 Identify the main clause in each of the following sentences:

    a Around 4.4 million listen on their mobile phone, up more than 25% on last year, with 1.8 million of them aged between 15 and 24.
    b Having seen off the rise of television music channels such as MTV in the 1980s, radio is now piggy backing on the digital revolution, with nearly 12 million people – 26% of the adult population – tuning in via digital radio, digital TV and the internet.
    c Another 2.7 million of us listen to podcasts downloaded on to our iPod or other MP3 player, up from 1.9 million.

Use of technical vocabulary

The writer uses a range of technical vocabulary specific to the subject. He takes for granted a level of knowledge in the reader. Some of the words he uses, such as those highlighted in the paragraph on the right, would mean nothing to a reader of fifty years ago or to someone who had no knowledge of the digital age.

In a world of ==digital TV==, video-on-demand and the ==iPod==, radio risked being left behind. There is something rather old-fashioned about switching on your 'wireless', a term more likely to refer to ==broadband internet== these days.

3 Re-read the article on page 102 and list other examples of technical vocabulary specific to the subject.

103

English: The Basic Skills

Use of personal pronouns

The journalist uses the personal pronouns 'we' and 'us' to make the readers feel as though the information is directly relevant to them, as in the sentence on the right.

But the latest audience figures published yesterday reveal that ==we== are more in love with the radio than ever before.

4 Identify two more places where the journalist uses personal pronouns in the article on page 102.

Accuracy

An article such as this would be carefully checked by both the writer and the newspaper editor to ensure that the meaning is clear and the grammar, punctuation and spelling are accurate.

5 The following paragraph contains eight errors.
   a Identify each error.
   b Number the errors 1 to 8 and write the corrected forms. Then check your answers by looking back at the original article.

Around 4.4 million listen on there mobile phone up more than 25% on last year, with 1.8 million of them aged between 15 and 24. 'In this multiplatform enviroment it's absolutely vital for radio stations to make content ... accessible on as many platforms as possibly, said Paul Jackson, cheif executive of virgin radio, which became the first to launch on 3G mobile phones in 2005.

Checkpoint

Look back through the work you have done so far in this unit. Write a rule for each of the following headings that would help someone who needs to write an article using complex information.

- Organisation
- Personal pronouns
- Complex sentences
- Accuracy.
- Vocabulary

Communicating complex information effectively

Complex information can be presented through charts and diagrams. Journalists often have to draw on information presented in this way when writing an article.

6 You are going to write an article on changes in internet use, based on the following. Your aim is to communicate the information clearly and effectively. Follow the steps A–H on page 105.

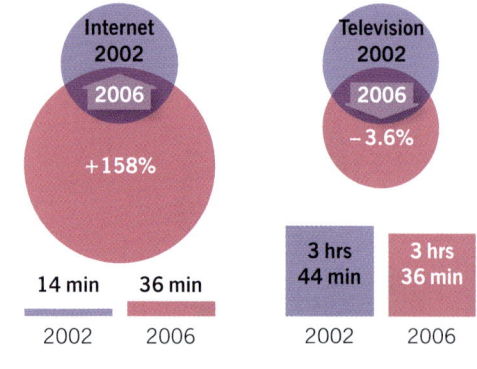

Internet 2002 / 2006 +158%
Television 2002 / 2006 −3.6%

How media use has changed
Percentage change in time spent per day on communication services (above)
Actual time spent (below)

14 min (2002)   36 min (2006)

3 hrs 44 min (2002)   3 hrs 36 min (2006)

The Guardian, 23 August 2007

24 Complex and clear

Women going online

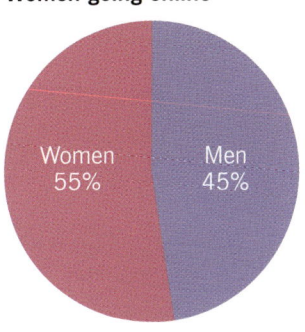

Women 55%
Men 45%

Women aged 25–34 spend more time online than men in the same age group

Web use by age
Average monthly online hours per user

Age	Hours
Under 12	30.5
12–17	24.9
18–24	37.9
25–34	29.0
35–49	32.1
50–64	33.5
65+	41.6

"Ever since it kicked off in the early 90s the web has been male-dominated. For the first time this year women are spending more time on the internet than men." (Peter Phillips, strategy and market developments partner at Ofcom, referring to users in the 25 to 49 age bracket)

What people go online for
% of households using the internet

Activity	%
Download music and video	43%
Play games online	30%
Social networking	23%
Video clips/webcasts	21%
Radio	21%
TV	9%

"The boom in web use is nothing new. But what website owners such as newspapers, TV companies and travel agents have to get to grips with is a new type of surfer."
(Katie Allen, Media business correspondent)

Key trends
- Britons are the most active web users in Europe and spend an average 36 minutes each online every day.
- Some 16% of over-65s use the web. They surf for 42 hours every month, more than any other age group. One quarter of UK web users are over 50.

The Guardian, 23 August 2007

A Study and make notes on the information presented to you. Highlight in your notes the details you are going to include.

B Decide on the best order for presenting the information to your readers and number your highlighted notes.

C Think about and make notes on how you will start your article. Your aim is to get your readers interested so that they will want to read on.

D Are there any conclusions you can draw from the information that will help your readers to understand it? If so, make a note of them and decide where you should put them in your article.

E Decide on an effective headline and final sentence.

F Write your article using a range of sentence structures, including complex ones.

G Make appropriate use of technical vocabulary and personal pronouns.

H Check your work carefully to make sure that your meaning is clear and your grammar, punctuation and spelling are accurate.

Group activity

7
a Work in groups of three or four. Read each other's articles and assess each one on how clearly and effectively the information is presented. Keep a record of your thoughts on each one.

b When you have read all the articles, take it in turns to say what you thought about each one.

c Decide between you which article was the best and for what reasons.

Summary

In this unit you have:
- examined the techniques writers use to communicate complex information clearly and effectively
- used graphs and diagrams to obtain relevant information
- written an informative article on a complex subject.

25 Persuasive powers

THE CHORLEY COURIER

ACME ART LIMITED
Pictures — we've got 'em

CHORLEY'S TRANSPORT HORROR

* TRAFFIC CHAOS
* COMMUTERS

The Editor
The Chorley Courier
PO Box 49
Chorley
Lancashire
PR19 7PO

14 Greyscales
Chorley
Lancashire
PR28 4JT

25 June 2008

Dear Editor

How would you like to start your day with the rain blasting through the broken windows of a vandalised bus shelter? Perhaps you would enjoy being squashed between a mother and toddler and a builder with B.O. for fifteen long minutes? Or maybe you'd relish the choking carbon dioxide fumes of fifty stationary cars outside your place of work? No? I thought not. But this is exactly what awaits many teenagers every day once they leave the comfort of their homes.

It's no joke. The state of public transport in Chorley is bad and getting worse. And it's because it's so bad that many parents feel compelled to drive their children to school or college, thus creating traffic problems and polluting the environment. If we are ever to tackle the problem of the 'school run', then we must first tackle the problems with our dilapidated bus service.

Modern, efficient buses are needed and plenty of them. Is that too much to ask for in the 21st century? Other countries seem to manage to get their children to school and college on time without taking the cars out of the garage. If they can do it, so can we.

All it needs is an organised campaign, supported by parents and other readers of this paper. Together we could make the difference. So come on, Chorley Courier, start the campaign right now. It's time to think about future generations and start going places.

Yours sincerely

Michael Jones

25 Persuasive powers

In this unit ...

you will identify the main purposes of a text and how it is organised and presented. You will then assess how well the writer makes his point. You will also plan and write a persuasive letter.

The letter on page 106 was sent to a local newspaper by a fifteen-year-old student. Read the letter carefully, then answer the questions below.

Identifying purpose

The **purpose** of a text is the reason for which it was written. A text may have more than one purpose.

1 Which of the following purposes do you think the writer had in mind when he wrote the letter? Give a reason for each one you choose.
  a to complain about his journey to school
  b to criticise parents who drive their children to school or college
  c to argue that the local bus service should be improved
  d to persuade adults to let children have the available seats on buses
  e to persuade the newspaper to start a campaign.

2 Now decide which is the *main* purpose of the text, out of the ones you have chosen. Give a reason for your decision.

Organising ideas

Many people write letters to newspapers. The ones that are chosen for printing need to be well organised.

The writer of this letter has organised his ideas in four paragraphs to get his points across clearly.

3 List the paragraphs P1 to P4. Decide which of the following summaries best describes each paragraph. Write the letter of the appropriate summary next to it:
  a states what is needed to sort out the problem
  b encourages paper to start a campaign
  c describes the current situation
  d links the problem with the buses to the problem with the 'school run'.

4 The openings of paragraphs two to four each continue a point made at the end of the previous paragraph.
  a Look at the panel below. Match the paragraph endings on the left to the correct following paragraph starters on the right.
  b For each one explain the link that is made.

1	But this is exactly what awaits many teenagers every day once they leave the comfort of their homes.	A	All it needs is an organised campaign ...
2	... we must first tackle the problems with our dilapidated bus service.	B	It's no joke.
3	If they can do it, so can we.	C	Modern, efficient buses are needed ...

107

English: The Basic Skills

5 With another student, discuss whether the writer's chosen order is the best order for communicating his ideas. If you think it is, explain why. If you think it is not, explain which order you would have chosen and why.

Making points effectively

The writer of the letter uses a range of techniques to make his points effectively and to persuade the reader.

These include using:

- personal pronouns such as *you* and *we*
- description
- rhetorical questions
- short sentences.

Sometimes, one or more of these techniques are used in the same sentence. For example:

'How would you like to start your day with the rain blasting through the broken windows of a vandalised bus shelter?'

This is a rhetorical question; it is asked for effect rather than to get an answer. It also addresses the reader directly as 'you' and describes the situation.

6 Find and write down one more example of each of the techniques listed in the bullet points on the left.

7 For each example you have chosen:
- explain the intended effect on the reader
- say whether you think it is effective or not and why.

8 The following paragraph was written as the opening of a letter to a newspaper about the problem of litter. Write a better opening paragraph using the four techniques you have examined. Your aim is to make it interesting and effective.

> I think there is far too much litter on the streets nowadays. Where I live there's lots of litter like cans and paper cartons and things like that. I'm really fed up with walking along and seeing other people's mess. Nobody seems to want to do anything about it except me and I don't know what to do.

Checkpoint

Read another student's opening paragraph. Check that they have used each of the four techniques.

Write one or two sentences to say how effective you think their paragraph is, giving the reasons for your opinion.

25 Persuasive powers

Writing your own letter

Remember, when writing a letter to a newspaper you need to:

- have a clear purpose or purposes in mind
- organise your ideas
- make your writing effective.

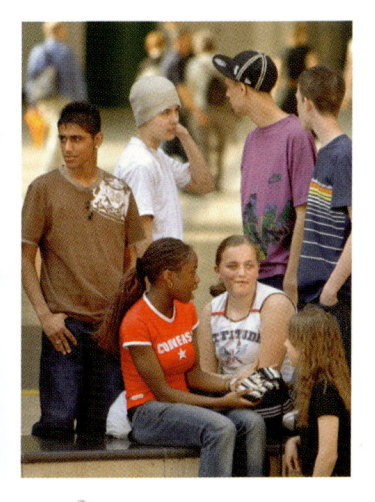

9 You are now going to write your own letter to a local newspaper. Your main purposes are:

- to show that there is not enough for young people to do in your area
- to suggest things that could be done to improve the situation
- to persuade the newspaper to start a campaign to improve the situation.

Follow these steps:

1. **Gather ideas**: list as many useful ideas as you can. You do not need to use them all in your writing but you can draw on them and you won't get stuck for ideas half way through.

2. **Organise your ideas into paragraphs**: decide which ideas you are going to use and the order in which you are going to write them. Aim to write three or four paragraphs. Make a paragraph plan.

3. **Think about how to make points effectively**: remind yourself of the techniques the writer of the letter on page 106 used to persuade his readers. Think about how you could best use those techniques for maximum effectiveness.

4. **Write your letter**: using the same format as the letter on page 106, write your letter. Reread each paragraph after writing it to make sure you have:

- made the point(s) you wanted to make
- used techniques to persuade your reader.

5. **Get a second opinion**: ask another student to read your letter and to list two things you do well and two things you could do to improve it.

6. **Make improvements**: make any changes to your letter that will make it more effective.

Checkpoint

You are going to assess your own writing by answering the following questions.

Have you set out your letter using the format of the letter on page 106 ?	Yes/No
Have you organised your ideas into three or four clear paragraphs?	Yes/No
Have you used personal pronouns such as *you* and *we*?	Yes/No
Have you used description?	Yes/No
Have you used rhetorical questions?	Yes/No
Have you used short sentences for effect?	Yes/No

On a scale of 1 to 6, where 1 is the poorest, what mark would you award your letter for overall effectiveness?

Give two reasons for your answer.

* ** *** **** ***** ******
1 ──────────────── 6

Summary

In this unit you have:

- learned about the main purposes of a text and how it is organised
- considered how well the writer makes his point
- planned and written your own persuasive letter.

109

26 Wild thoughts

I was in South Georgia the day after the northern bottlenose whale swam up the River Thames. From afar, it appeared to me that our nation of animal-lovers excelled itself in its interest and concern. Thousands gathered along London's riverbanks as the attempt to save the frightened young whale was beamed across the globe by TV crews.

The odds were always against a bottlenose whale surviving in the Thames and the valiant rescue effort ultimately failed. But it did demonstrate a mind-boggling level of compassion.

So why aren't we mourning the deaths of thousands of whales being killed every year by Iceland, Norway and Japan? The whaling situation is getting worse, and full-scale commercial whaling could restart before the end of the decade. Why does a single whale get more publicity than that?

The fact is that it's much harder to grasp the predicament of an entire population or species than that of an individual animal. That is why the only argument that will ever make a difference in the public mind is the sheer cruelty involved.

Just a few days after the bottlenose whale died, Japanese whalers announced the invention of a new super-harpoon that explodes and hurls shards of metal through a whale's body. It will be used to kill humpback and fin whales and is being tested on live whales right now.

Meanwhile Greenpeace has released footage of Japan's whale hunt in the Southern Ocean Whale Sanctuary. The video shows a harpoon exploding inside a whale's back. The animal is winched up to the ship alive and struggles in agony for 10 minutes before dying.

If only whales could scream. Maybe then the rest of the world would wake up and listen!

Mark Carwardine, BBC Wildlife Magazine, April 2006

26 Wild thoughts

In this unit ...

You will read a text in detail and examine the writer's point of view. You will also discuss issues raised by the text.

In January 2006 a seven-tonne whale made its way up the Thames to central London, where it was watched by riverside crowds. Despite the efforts to save her she died the next day. Read the article on the opposite page, which was written in response to the huge amount of public support for the whale.

Key points

When making a case for or against something, writers present the reader with an argument. To develop the argument writers use key points to build up their case bit by bit.

1 In **Wild thoughts** the writer makes a series of key points listed below:
   a If we could hear the whales we might listen to them.
   b It's easier to care for one whale than for thousands.
   c Tests are taking place on more powerful harpoons.
   d The whale's death showed how much people cared.
   e Harpoons cause whales to die in great agony.
   f Britain is a nation of animal lovers.
   g People don't seem to care about the deaths of thousands of whales.

Copy and complete the following table, placing the key points in the order that they appear in the article. The first one has been done for you.

1	2	3	4	5	6	7
f						

Fact and opinion

The writer uses facts and opinions to support the key points.

A fact is something which can be proved to be true.

An opinion is a point of view which cannot be proved to be true or untrue.

2 Decide whether the following are fact or opinion:
   a It appeared to me that our nation of animal-lovers excelled itself in its interest and concern.
   b That is why the only argument that will ever make a difference in the public mind is the sheer cruelty involved.
   c It will be used to kill humpback and fin whales and is being tested on live whales right now.
   d The video shows a harpoon exploding inside a whale's back.

3 Just because a writer says something is a fact, doesn't mean it is:

> The fact is that it's much harder to grasp the predicament of an entire population or species than that of an individual animal.

   a Is the above sentence fact or opinion? Explain why.
   b Give two reasons which would explain why a writer would present an opinion as though it were a fact.

111

English: The Basic Skills

4 What facts and/or opinions in the article are used to support the following key points?

a Britain is a nation of animal-lovers.
b It's easier to care for one whale than for thousands.
c Tests are taking place on more powerful harpoons.
d Harpoons cause whales to die in great agony.

Checkpoint

Compare your answers to questions 1 to 4 with a partner's. Where you have different answers, decide who is right.

Copy and complete these sentences:

A writer will develop an argument by making a series of _____.

A fact is _____.

An opinion is _____.

Writers sometimes present opinions as facts because _____.

Emotive use of language

Writers often choose words to influence the feelings of the reader. This is called emotive use of language.

5 Read the following sentence:

> Thousands gathered along London's riverbanks as the attempt to save the frightened young whale was beamed across the globe by TV crews.

a Which word is used to influence the reader's feelings?
b What is the writer hoping to make the reader feel?

6 Read the following sentence:

> The odds were always against a **bottlenose** whale surviving in the Thames and the valiant rescue effort ultimately failed.

a What does the word 'valiant' suggest?
b Why do you think the writer has used this word?

The writer's point of view

You have worked out how the writer:

• uses facts and opinions to build an argument

• uses words to influence the reader.

These both tell you things about the writer's point of view.

7 What have you worked out so far about the writer's attitude to whaling?

8 To develop your understanding of the writer's attitude to whaling you need to ask questions both about what you are told and what you are not told.
An example of a question you could ask is:

Were the people visiting the Thames really compassionate or were they just curious?

Write one or two more questions to ask the writer.

26 **Wild thoughts**

Pair activity

9 With a partner, choose **three** of the following statements which **best show** the writer's point of view. Use evidence from the text to explain why you have chosen each one.
- He wants the reader to feel sorry for the stranded whale.
- He believes whaling (hunting and killing whales) should be stopped.
- He believes people don't care about whales.
- He believes whaling is cruel.
- He wants people to protest against whaling.

Developing your point of view

In **Wild thoughts** the writer puts forward the view that whaling is cruel and people should do more to stop it.

10 Read and think about the following information.

> Blue whales, which are twice the size of the largest dinosaur that ever roamed the planet and swim in U.S. waters, numbered 250,000 in 1920 but have declined by 96 percent since then. Fin whales, which used to number 600,000, have declined by 92 percent.
>
> www.washingtonpost.com

> Approximately 750,000,000 animals and 650,000 tons of fish are slaughtered each year for food in Britain. Farm animals are stunned by electricity or percussion, and killed by cutting the blood vessels in the neck. Fish caught at sea or by anglers die of asphyxia, when they are taken out of the water.
>
> www.hedweb.com

How does what you have just read develop your thinking about:
- whaling
- killing animals for food?

Group activity

In a group you are going to discuss the question: "Should people kill animals for food or other products?"

Your aims are to present your ideas clearly and to take part in the discussion.

11 Follow these steps:
- Choose two or three people to work with.
- Make your own notes outlining what you think. Include evidence to support the things you want to say. You could use 'Wild thoughts', the extra information in question 10, and your own knowledge and experience.
- In turn, explain your ideas to the group. Aim to present your ideas clearly and try to persuade the others to think as you do by using words emotively as the writer of 'Wild thoughts' does.
- After everyone has spoken, allow time for further questions and discussion.
- At the end of the discussion, choose the person you think was most effective in presenting their ideas and taking part in the discussion. List three to five reasons to explain why you chose them.

Summary

In this unit you have:
- identified the main points and ideas in a text
- examined the writer's point of view
- developed and clearly presented your own point of view, including the use of fact and opinion and use of emotive language.

27 Improving your writing

In this unit ...

you will develop your skills in one of the final stages of writing: proofreading and revising. This is when you make your writing as good as it possibly can be.

There are various stages in the process of writing between the start and the finish. These are listed below.

1 Planning: working out purpose, audience, content, style and order.

2 Writing the first draft: your first attempt to get your ideas down according to your plan.

3 Re-drafting: re-reading and changing your first draft to make improvements.

4 Proofreading and revising: checking your re-draft for accuracy, clarity and language.

5 Writing the final draft: putting it all together in the finished piece of writing.

When you are doing stage 4, **proofreading and revising**, you need to think about:

- correcting errors in grammar, punctuation and spelling
- making sure your meaning is clear
- matching your language to your audience and purpose
- making your writing as effective as it can be for its audience and purpose.

Correcting errors

Here is the opening paragraph of a piece written by a student (Paragraph A). In it, he gives his views on why driving lessons should be provided at school or college.

1 Read Paragraph A carefully and identify where you need to:
- correct the spelling
- correct the punctuation.

Paragraph A

If kids were learnt to drive at school then it would proberbly be better for everyone. Firstly since most young people have proberbly decided they want to drive some might not even bother to take the driving test. They will just get a car and get on with it. One of the resons for them driving without a license could be that they cant afford the lessons, which if they had at school for free wouldnt be a problem and might encourage more people to learn first. Also if they were learning in a class with their mates it might make them more open to the idea.

27 Improving your writing

2 Copy the following paragraph from the same student's work (Paragraph B). You will be working on it in questions 3–5. Leave a line between each line of your writing so that you will have room to make corrections, like this:

> taught   opportunities
> If they are ~~learnt~~ at school they will have more ~~oppertunitys~~
>
> to learn.

Paragraph B

If they are learnt at school they will have more oppertunitys to learn. Its not just like now how every weak they don't like what they are doing, it might even get them in school more. If the kids where taught to drive whilst they were still in school it might be easier for them to go out and get a job when they leave school with a car so basiclly why shouldnt kids be able to learn to drive at school. It is safer for other people helps people who cant afford the lessons and might help kids for when they leave school so why haven't these lessons already started.

3 Correct the grammar, spelling and punctuation in Paragraph B. Use the example in question 2 to get you started.

Making the meaning clear

When proofreading and revising, you should also aim to make the meaning as clear as possible. On the right is an example of changes that could be made to Paragraph A to make the meaning clearer.

> reasons   licence
> One of the resons for them driving without a license
>   can't   move highlighted text to here
> could be that they cant afford the lessons, which | if they
> insert **them** to make clearer   wouldn't
> had | at school for free <mark>wouldnt be a problem</mark> and might
>
> encourage more people to learn first. Also | if they were
>
> learning in a class with their mates | it might make them
>   insert: **of taking lessons** for clarity
> more open to the idea |.

4 Make any further changes to your corrected copy of Paragraph B that you think will make the meaning clearer.

115

English: The Basic Skills

Matching language to audience.

Another part of improving your writing is to make sure that the language you use is appropriate for your purpose and audience. Paragraph A was written for the governors of a school. The language should be formal. Below is an example of some changes to the text to make the language used match the intended audience.

> change to students   change to taught
> If ~~kids~~ were ~~learnt~~ to drive at school ... Also if they were
> change to friends
> learning in a class with their ~~mates~~ it might make them
> more open to the idea of taking lessons.

5 Make any further changes to your corrected copy of Paragraph B that you think are needed to match the language to the intended audience. Remember, you need to make sure that the language is *formal*.

Checkpoint

Compare your final paragraph with a partner's.
Decide whose version is the better, and why. Then make any further helpful changes to your own writing.

Making your writing effective

Once you have corrected for accuracy, meaning and language, your writing should be looking good. But there is one more thing to think about: you need to aim to make your writing as *effective* as it can be.

6 a Read the following paragraph written by a student aiming to persuade others to adopt a healthier lifestyle. Think about the changes you could make to improve it.

> Key Facts topic of the day is Fitness. Nowadays more and more people are suffering with major health scares and problems as a result of being over-weight, and generally thus meaning that people are very unfit. Us at Key Facts think this is a very serious and have used the very intelligent internet to research some key facts just to outline the large seriousness of this.

b Study the following revisions closely.

> **Key Facts – Fitness**
>
> Today's topic of the day is Fitness. Nowadays more and more people are suffering ~~with~~ problems and major health scares ~~and~~ problems as a direct result of being over-weight and, even more seriously, ~~generally thus meaning that people are very unfit~~ having low levels of fitness. ~~Us~~ We at Key Facts ~~think~~ consider this ~~is~~ to be a very serious issue. ~~and have used the very intelligent internet to~~ With the help of internet research, we have unearthed some key facts ~~just~~ to help outline the extreme seriousness of this issue.

27 Improving your writing

c Identify and list the changes that have been made and how they improve the paragraph. You could do this in a table – copy and complete the one below.

Changes	Effects
Opening sentence changed into a sub-heading and a sentence.	Makes the subject clear and the opening sharper and more precise.

7 The changes made to the above passage are mainly concerned with:
- changing sentence structures to create more variety and greater pace
- changing words to show a more mature and effective vocabulary range.

a Read the rest of this student's writing below.

b Think carefully about the changes you might make and the things you might want to keep as they are.

c Once you have thought about it, write your revised version.

Over 40% of our population is currently overweight and 15% obese. Also we are one of the most unfit countries in Europe today, and if we carry on this way most young people at this present time won't be around for their 60th birthdays.

Setting aside these facts, we all in our heart of hearts know that eating healthily and good fitness levels are the key to a better lifestyle and longer life expectancy, but we all seem to think that we can sort it with the click of a finger. I bet everyone listening now at some point has been on a diet and most of the time has found it didn't work and self-esteem and motivation has been lost to try again. Even when we do pluck up the courage to do something about our weight or fitness the same old phrase is said, I'll start tomorrow or I'll definitely start on Monday this really meaning I can't be bothered to start today, what difference will another day or two matter?

Well in answer to that, the difference could be life changing. Why not start today? You never know what's around tomorrow's corner.

---

8 List the changes you have made and the effects of these. You could use a table like the one in question 6.

Checkpoint

Compare your revised writing with a partner's. Decide which one is better and why. In your table, note any further changes you could make to improve your revision.

Summary

In this unit you have:
- considered how to revise writing in order to make it more accurate, appropriate and effective
- looked at other students' writing to learn the skills you need to revise your own writing to make it as good as it can possibly be.

28 Why wear fur?

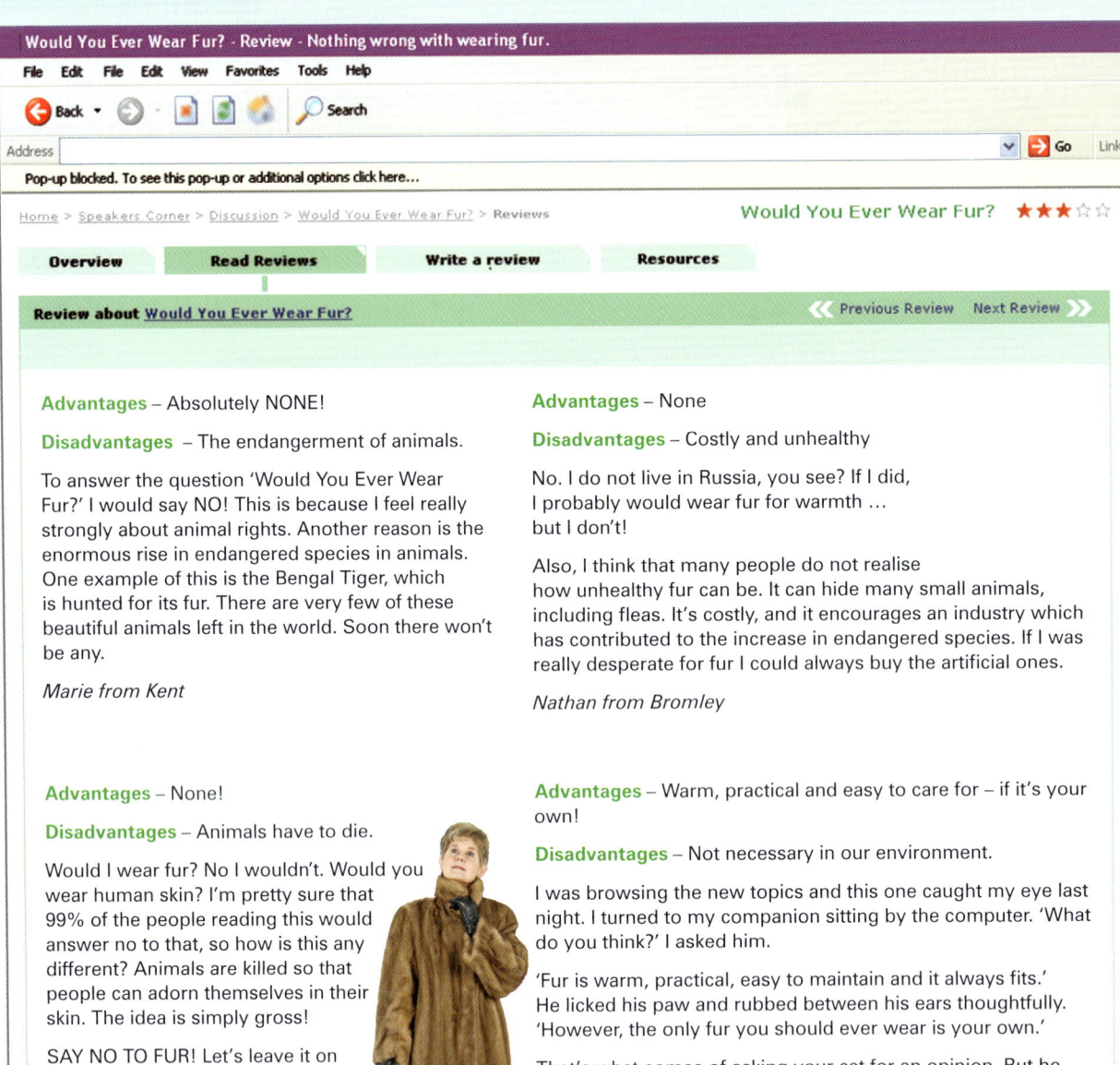

Would You Ever Wear Fur? - Review - Nothing wrong with wearing fur.

Home > Speakers Corner > Discussion > Would You Ever Wear Fur? > Reviews

Would You Ever Wear Fur? ★★★☆☆

Overview | Read Reviews | Write a review | Resources

Review about Would You Ever Wear Fur?   « Previous Review   Next Review »

Advantages – Absolutely NONE!

Disadvantages – The endangerment of animals.

To answer the question 'Would You Ever Wear Fur?' I would say NO! This is because I feel really strongly about animal rights. Another reason is the enormous rise in endangered species in animals. One example of this is the Bengal Tiger, which is hunted for its fur. There are very few of these beautiful animals left in the world. Soon there won't be any.

Marie from Kent

Advantages – None

Disadvantages – Costly and unhealthy

No. I do not live in Russia, you see? If I did, I probably would wear fur for warmth … but I don't!

Also, I think that many people do not realise how unhealthy fur can be. It can hide many small animals, including fleas. It's costly, and it encourages an industry which has contributed to the increase in endangered species. If I was really desperate for fur I could always buy the artificial ones.

Nathan from Bromley

Advantages – None!

Disadvantages – Animals have to die.

Would I wear fur? No I wouldn't. Would you wear human skin? I'm pretty sure that 99% of the people reading this would answer no to that, so how is this any different? Animals are killed so that people can adorn themselves in their skin. The idea is simply gross!

SAY NO TO FUR! Let's leave it on the animal. After all, they are the ones who look best in it!

Jackie from Swansea

Advantages – Warm, practical and easy to care for – if it's your own!

Disadvantages – Not necessary in our environment.

I was browsing the new topics and this one caught my eye last night. I turned to my companion sitting by the computer. 'What do you think?' I asked him.

'Fur is warm, practical, easy to maintain and it always fits.' He licked his paw and rubbed between his ears thoughtfully. 'However, the only fur you should ever wear is your own.'

That's what comes of asking your cat for an opinion. But he has a point. If we as human beings actually NEEDED fur, we'd grow it. Evolution has left us with very little fur. So we can conclude that most of us don't need it. Nothing good can come from wearing fur.

Becky from Glasgow

28 Why wear fur?

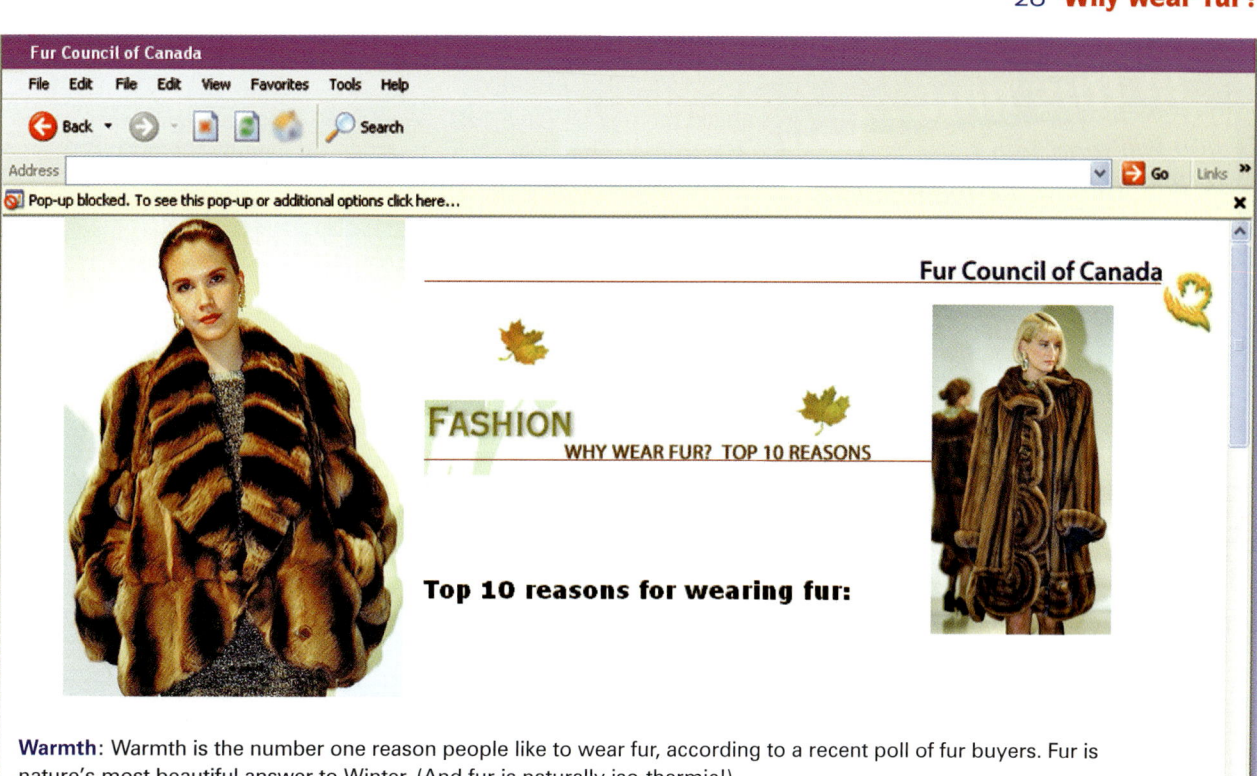

Fur Council of Canada

FASHION
WHY WEAR FUR? TOP 10 REASONS

Top 10 reasons for wearing fur:

Warmth: Warmth is the number one reason people like to wear fur, according to a recent poll of fur buyers. Fur is nature's most beautiful answer to Winter. (And fur is naturally iso-thermic!)

Fashion: Modern, casual or elegant, fur is always in style. More than 300 top international designers are now using fur in their collections. Hip hop artists, pop singers and other celebs have made fur a hot trend with younger people.

Long-lasting: Fur is a naturally durable fibre that lasts for many, many years. (The synthetics that animal activists would have us wear are usually made from petroleum – a non-renewable resource that can cause serious pollution problems. Oil spills aren't great for wildlife!)

Re-styleable: Unlike other clothing materials, your fur can be updated and re-styled to reflect the latest fashions, time and time again. That's ecological! (How many other clothes can be used and re-used for 30 years or more?)

Environmentally friendly: A fine natural product, fur is bio-degradable and a renewable resource. In fact, "the sustainable use of wildlife" is now promoted by the World Wildlife Fund, the World Conservation Union (IUCN) and every major conservation organisation.

Versatile: Fur can be worn for all occasions. Whether with jeans or an evening gown, wearing fur will make you look and feel terrific! With lighter weight fur and new techniques, fur apparel and accessories are now an all-season fashion.

Supporting livelihoods and cultures: When you buy fur, you support thousands of aboriginal and other people living close to the land – people who have a direct interest in protecting vital wildlife habitat. Most of us eat meat and wear leather; in northern Canada there are no cows – there are muskrats and beavers, which are eaten by aboriginal and other hunters. Should they throw away the fur, which is one of the few resources they have for their livelihoods?

Responsible conservation: Furs used in the trade are abundant. Strict national and international controls (e.g., CITES) ensure that NO endangered species are ever used. A commitment to animal welfare is also assured by state and provincial regulations.

Supporting farm families: Many furs (especially mink, fox and chinchilla) are now raised on farms. These animals receive excellent nutrition and treatment; there is no other way to produce the quality of fur required.

Fur is your choice!: If you do choose to wear fur, it's good to know that the fur trade is a responsible, well-regulated industry. So long as 95% of the population eats meat, why shouldn't we enjoy the comfort and beauty of fur?

furisgreen.com

© Fur Council of Canada

English: The Basic Skills

In this unit ...

you will read two texts in detail to understand the main points they are making and to find specific information. You will then compare the organisation, presentation and content of the two texts and discuss the issues raised in them.

Read the text on page 118, 'Would you ever wear fur?', then answer the following multiple-choice questions to identify the main points the writers are making.

1 Which of the following reasons does Marie give to explain why she wouldn't wear fur?
   a Fur looks better on animals.
   b The enormous rise in endangered animal species.
   c Fur is costly.

Understanding the main points

To develop your skills as a reader you need to read texts closely so that you understand the main points the writer or writers are making.

2 Which of the following reasons does Nathan give to explain why he wouldn't wear fur?
   a Fur won't keep you warm.
   b Animals need the fur for themselves.
   c Fur can be full of fleas.

3 How does Jackie describe the idea of wearing fur?
   a People look their best in it.
   b It's simply gross.
   c Fur can be unhealthy.

4 Why is Becky opposed to wearing fur?
   a It's not practical or easy to care for.
   b She doesn't want to wear cat fur.
   c It's not necessary in our environment.

Finding specific information

Sometimes when you read you need to identify and select specific points made in a text. To do this you need to read the text closely.

Read carefully the text on page 119, 'Top 10 reasons for wearing fur'. Then answer the following question.

5 Five of the following claims are made in 'Top 10 reasons for wearing fur'. Identify the correct five.
   a Furs used in the trade are abundant.
   b Fur is bio-degradable.
   c Fur is very expensive.
   d Fur should only be worn on formal occasions.
   e Fur is a fine natural product.
   f Fur is always in style.
   g Fur is taken from endangered species.
   h Fur can be updated and re-styled.

28 Why wear fur?

> **Checkpoint**
>
> Check your answers to questions 1 to 5 with another student's. Where you have different answers, go back to the questions and decide who is right.

Organisation and presentation

The two texts on pages 118 and 119 are taken from different websites. Both texts use a title and sub-headings to organise the content.

6 a Identify and write down the title of each text.

b Which one addresses the reader directly? Why does it do this?

7 Both texts use sub-headings.

a What is the function of the sub-headings in the 'Would you ever wear fur?' text?

b What is the function of the sub-headings in the 'Top 10 reasons for wearing fur' text?

Summarising ideas

In 'Top 10 reasons for wearing fur' the sub-heading summarises in one or a few words the sentences that follow it.

In 'Would you ever wear fur?' the sub-headings 'Advantages' and 'Disadvantages' give the writers the opportunity to summarise their views. Sometimes the writer uses a key word or key words from the passage itself.

> **Fashion:** Modern, casual or elegant, fur is always in style. More than 300 top international designers are now using fur in their collections. Hip hop artists, pop singers and other celebs have made fur a hot trend with younger people.

> **Advantages** – None
>
> **Disadvantages** – Costly and unhealthy
>
> No. I do not live in Russia, you see? If I did, I probably would wear fur for warmth … but I don't!
>
> Also, I think that many people do not realise how **unhealthy** fur can be. It can hide many small animals, including fleas. It's **costly**, and it encourages an industry which has contributed to the increase in endangered species. If I was really desperate for fur I could always buy the artificial ones.

8 a Pick out the key words from the response on the right, which was also given to the question 'Would you ever wear fur?'

b Write your own 'Disadvantages' sub-heading for the response using the key words.

> I would NEVER wear fur. I think it is cruel and completely unnecessary!
>
> I cannot understand how people can drape a dead animal around them without feeling guilt that an animal, a wonderful life, had died. I think it is outrageous for models to wear fur with no pity or regard for the poor animals made into the item.

> **Checkpoint**
>
> Compare your sub-heading with a partner's.
> Decide which sub-heading best summarises the views of the writer and why.

English: The Basic Skills

Comparing content

When you compare the content of two texts you focus on the similarities and/or the differences in what they say. These two texts present a range of reasons why a person should or should not wear fur.

9 Look at the following table. The five points in the first column are made in 'Would you ever wear fur?' Copy and complete the table by finding points in 'Top 10 reasons for wearing fur' which present either a similar or a different view on the same subject. Make a note of whether a view is similar or different. The first one is done for you.

Would you ever wear fur?	Top 10 reasons for wearing fur
1 The idea is simply gross!	1 … wearing fur will make you look and feel terrific! (different)
2 If I did [live in Russia], I probably would wear fur for warmth …	2
3 … it encourages an industry which has contributed to the increase in endangered species.	3
4 After all, they [animals] are the ones who look best in it!	4
5 Nothing good can come from wearing fur.	5

Writing a comparison

When you write a comparison you need to connect the point made in one text with the point made in the other text and comment on it.

Words and phrases can be used to link the points. On the right are two examples and some other useful words and phrases.

In the first article one writer states that wearing fur is 'simply gross'. However, in the second article the writer suggests that wearing fur is a positive experience and 'will make you look and feel terrific!'

Both texts give opinions on wearing fur. In the first article it states that wearing fur is 'simply gross', whereas in the second article it suggests the wearer will 'look and feel terrific'. This creates a more positive impression.

- in contrast
- but
- similarly
- alternatively
- a similar point is made in

10 Take points 2 to 5 from the table you completed for question 9. Write sentences that *compare* the views expressed in both texts. Use the examples and the useful words and phrases above to help you.

Checkpoint

Complete these sentences to review what you have learned:

When you compare the content of two texts you …

When you write a comparison you need to …

Useful words and phrases for comparison include …

28 Why wear fur?

Developing your own point of view

You have read a range of opinions on the subject of wearing fur. Now you are going to develop your own views on this subject and take part in a discussion.

Group activity

11 In groups you are going to discuss the question: 'Should people wear fur?'

Before you get into groups:

- Re-read the articles and jot down the points you think are relevant to the question and whether you agree with them or not.
- Add any points of your own that were not made in the articles, and explain why they are relevant to the question.
- Study the images on this page and add any further points that these suggest to you.
- In one sentence, summarise your *personal* point of view on the question: 'Should people wear fur?'
- If you have time, do further research on the internet or in the library.

Now get into groups of three or four:

- Take it in turns to explain your point of view on the question 'Should people wear fur?' to the others in your group. Each person should speak for no more than one minute. Your aim is to present your ideas clearly and to explain why you think as you do.
- As each person speaks, the others should make notes on what they say.
- After everyone has spoken, each member of the group has one minute to question the others on their points of view.
- Look back at the one-sentence summary you wrote earlier. Think about the points other people in your group have made. Has anything been said to change your mind? If so, rewrite your sentence, summarising your new point of view.

Checkpoint

At the end of the discussion, award yourself a mark out of three for how well you:

- presented and explained your ideas (1 to 3)
- questioned other members of the group on their ideas. (1 to 3)

Now award a mark out of three for how each of the other members of your group did these.

Compare the total mark you gave yourself with the total mark given to you by other members of the group. What can you learn from any differences in the marks awarded?

Summary

In this unit you have:

- identified the main points of a text and found specific information
- thought about the use of sub-headings
- compared the ideas in two texts
- developed your own point of view.

Punctuation 1
Punctuation basics

C T F B . . ? ? ? ! ! !

Why do we need to use punctuation when we write?

Read the extract on the right and suggest reasons to explain why we use punctuation.

> the cumberland pencil museum is the only attraction in the world devoted exclusively to the rich and fascinating history of the pencil the museum charts the development of the humble pencil through the centuries the museum is the perfect all weather attraction near the centre of keswick and has its own free parking

You probably worked out that punctuation makes it easier for the reader to follow the writing.

You are now going to look at how to punctuate sentences using:
- capital letters
- full stops
- question marks
- exclamation marks.

Capital letters

Capital letters are used for a range of different reasons.

- At the start of each sentence
  > He asked her where the nearest shop was. She told him it was about two miles further on.

- For the personal pronoun 'I'
  > If I arrive early I'll get the caretaker to unlock the door.

- For the first letter of proper nouns (people's names, place names, names of days and months)
  > On Tuesday Karen went to Newcastle but found out the shop she wanted didn't open until September.

- For the first letter of titles of people and organisations
  > They asked the Head Teacher, Mrs Clasper, to attend the meeting with Social Services.

- For people's initials and abbreviations
  > Here are Dr and Mrs Husain from the USA.

- At the beginning of a new piece of direct speech
  > Sadly, he replied, "They didn't tell us where they were going".

- For the main words in titles of books, plays, games, films, etc
  > He thought that 'The Lord of the Rings' was still the best film he'd seen.

1 This extract from an ActionAid report on AIDS in Malawi has all the correct punctuation apart from capital letters.

Rewrite the extract placing capital letters where needed.

ActionAid contains two capital letters.

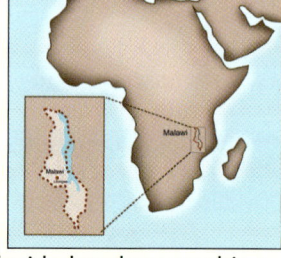

> nestled towards the southeast coast of africa, malawi is a beautiful but poor country. it suffers recurring food insecurity and has a devastating hiv and aids epidemic. an estimated one million people – around 15% of the population – are currently living with a virus that kills 90,000 malawians every year.
>
> in 2002, when actionaid supporter les pratt became aware of the crisis gripping the country, he decided to do something about it. "i saw television coverage of actionaid's work in malawi on hiv and aids," he says. "the work seemed to fit with what i felt were important issues to address, and it prompted me to make that first call that would become 'mission malawi'."
>
> *Common Cause 2007*

Punctuation 1 **Punctuation basics**

2 Thirty-three capital letters were needed to correct the ActionAid passage. Check your work and see if you identified all of them. If not, try again.

Full stops

The main use of a full stop is to mark the end of a sentence.

> The alley was dark and narrow and full of shadows. The children crept nervously through it.

If you don't use full stops to correctly punctuate sentences, readers will find it very difficult to follow what you have written.

3 The following paragraph contains six sentences. The sentences have no capital letters at the start and no full stops at the end of them. Read the paragraph through first to make sense of it and to identify the six sentences.

> leeches are segmented worms with a sucker at each end forest species hang by their rear sucker when a victim brushes past, they catch hold using the front sucker and start feeding leeches that feed on humans are common in rainforests in India they come out during the monsoon leeches usually fall off after feeding, but can attach themselves inside the nostrils of animals and, more rarely, to people who drink from streams
>
> BBC Wildlife Magazine, April 2006

Now rewrite the paragraph using capital letters and full stops in the correct places.

4 Read your punctuated version aloud. It should make clear sense. If it does not, you need to rethink where you have placed your punctuation marks.

Question marks and exclamation marks

There are two other punctuation marks which can be used at the end of a sentence.

? The question mark is used to mark the end of a question.

> How old are you? Who is that girl sitting at the back?

! The exclamation mark is used to show expression. It may mark the end of a sentence.

> Get out now!

! The exclamation mark may also be used at the end of an interjection.

> Oh no!

QUICK TEST

Decide which of the following sentences should end in a full stop, a question mark or an exclamation mark. Explain your choices to another student.

> Have you ever read a book you just couldn't put down_ Well, if not, you need to try Smokescreen_ It's the action book with everything needed to keep you on the edge of your seat until the very last page_ Like all the other books in this series, this one's a winner_ Read it now_

125

Punctuation 2
Commas

Commas make it easier for the reader to make sense of a sentence. In this unit you will learn and practise some basic rules for how to use commas.

Commas to separate items on a list

When you are writing lists in a sentence you need to separate the items with commas. The final comma, before the 'and', is usually left out.

For example:

> If you ever explore this area you will discover that you can go swimming, play football on the green or in the sports centre, visit a range of shops on the High Street and take advantage of the multiplex cinema.

1 Copy the following sentences. Place commas between the items in the list to make the sentences easier to follow.

> He opened the bag warily and inside found a crumpled note a rusty key some foreign coins a faded photograph and a suspicious-looking parcel.

> Anti-virus software is provided to protect computers against infected files provide support systems and automatically update virus definitions.

Commas to mark off extra information

When you give extra information about something or somebody, you use commas to separate it from the main sentence.

For example:

> Alf Johnson, 32, claimed he had bought the car the day before. Mr Johnson, a father of four, was unable to show a receipt and Judge Christine Carr, sitting at Lincoln County Court, found him guilty of theft.

2 Copy the following sentences. Underline the words that give you extra information and put commas around them.

> The street watched in wonder when Charlie Sooner the well-known local hero was up to his tricks again. This time Charlie climbed a tree to rescue his neighbour's cat. Mrs Elkin Charlie's neighbour for 27 years had called for help when her cat Pingu got stuck up a tree. Charlie war veteran 82 and grandfather of five didn't hesitate.

Punctuation 2 **Commas**

Checkpoint

Compare your answers to 1 and 2 with a partner. Where you have different answers, decide who is right and make the appropriate corrections.

Commas to separate off different parts of a sentence

Commas help the reader to make sense of what you have written. They mark a pause, the same way as you would pause when speaking. Say the following sentence aloud.

> Although the bus was late he still got to school on time.

To make clear sense of the sentence, you need to pause after *late*, so that is where you place your comma:

> Although the bus was late, he still got to school on time.

3 With a partner, read the following sentences aloud. Decide where commas should be placed.

> He still got there on time even though the bus was late.

> To complete the form properly you must use a black pen.

> Having set the alarm incorrectly Carl was very late for work.

> Before you open the gate make sure the dog is in the kennel.

LEARN

The best ways to learn how to use commas well are to:

- take notice of how other writers use them
- read your writing aloud to help you work out where you need to pause to make sense of it. Decide whether you need to place a comma at this spot.

QUICK TEST

Read the following extract from a computer manual. Notice how the commas have been used to help the reader follow the meaning.

> Your computer can catch a virus from disks, a local network, or the Internet. Just as a cold virus attaches itself to a human host, a computer virus attaches itself to a program. And just like a cold, it is contagious. Like viruses, worms replicate themselves. However, instead of spreading from file to file, they spread from computer to computer, infecting an entire system.

Write a paragraph that could be used in a manual or guide. It can be based on a thing or a place you know something about. Aim to write 60–70 words and to use sentences that need commas.

Swap your passage with a partner. Read each passage aloud in turn. Are the commas in the correct places? After discussion, make any changes you think are necessary.

Punctuation 3
Apostrophes

Apostrophes are often used incorrectly, but they are actually quite straightforward. Once you know how and when to use them properly, you will come across all kinds of examples where someone has got it wrong!

The apostrophe has two uses:
- to show where one or more letters have been missed out (omission)
- to show that something belongs to someone or something (possession).

Using apostrophes for omission

Instead of saying 'I am', we often use the shortened form of 'I'm'. The apostrophe is used in writing to show that a letter, or letters have been missed out.

For example:

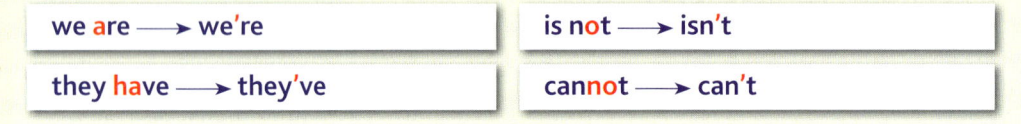

| we are ⟶ we're | is not ⟶ isn't |
| they have ⟶ they've | cannot ⟶ can't |

The apostrophe is placed in the exact spot where the missing letter or letters would have appeared.

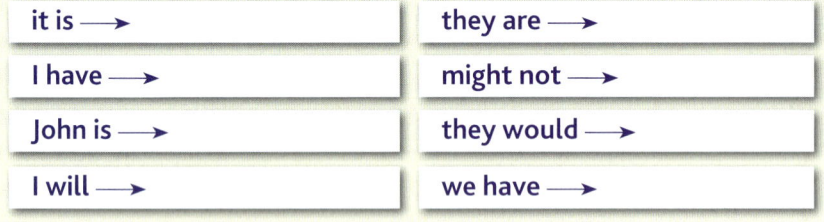

1 Copy and complete the following:

it is ⟶	they are ⟶
I have ⟶	might not ⟶
John is ⟶	they would ⟶
I will ⟶	we have ⟶

Check your answers with a partner before moving on.

> **LEARN**
>
> There are a few commonly used words that don't follow the normal rule and you should learn these:
> - *will not* becomes *won't*
> - *shall not* becomes *shan't*

2 Copy and complete the following message. Use apostrophes to shorten the underlined words.

Check your answers with a partner before moving on.

> <u>I would</u> really like to join you on your birthday. Unfortunately, <u>I have</u> a meeting planned for the same date. Hopefully, <u>I will</u> be able to leave a bit early so it <u>should not</u> be too late to meet up with you. <u>It will</u> be good to see you again. Hope <u>you are</u> keeping well and <u>have not</u> had too many problems with work.

> **QUICK TEST**
>
> Devise your own test of 10 questions on the use of apostrophe for omission. Make it as difficult as you like, but make sure you have the correct answers written separately before giving your test to a partner to complete.
>
> Check their answers against your own.

Punctuation 3 **Apostrophes**

Using apostrophes for possession

We rarely say 'the house of my friend'. We would be more likely to say 'my friend's house'. In this case the apostrophe is used to show that the house belongs to the friend. The friend is the possessor. Where you place the apostrophe depends on whether the possessor is singular or plural.

Singular

When the possessor is singular, as in the case of 'Paul', the apostrophe is placed after the word and an 's' is added.

For example: the friend of Paul ⟶ Paul's friend

3 Copy and complete the following:

the daughter of the woman ⟶   the passengers of the boat ⟶

Check your answers with a partner before moving on.

Plural, ending in 's'

When the possessor is plural and already ends in an 's', we just add an apostrophe.

For example: the school of the girls ⟶ the girls' school

> **LEARN**
> Note that the possessive words 'yours', 'his', 'hers', 'its', 'ours' and 'theirs' are <u>not</u> written with an apostrophe.

4 Copy and complete the following:

the football kits of the boys ⟶   the staffroom of the teachers ⟶

Check your answers with a partner before moving on.

Plural, not ending in 's'

When the possessor is plural but does not end in an 's', we add an apostrophe and an 's'.

For example: the toilets of the men ⟶ the men's toilets

5 Copy and complete the following:

the homes of the women ⟶   the toys of the children ⟶

Check your answers with a partner before moving on.

> **LEARN**
> It is important to remember that **it's** should only have an apostrophe when short for **it is**. When it is used possessively (belonging to), **it** becomes **its** and has no apostrophe.

QUICK TEST

The following passage should contain seven apostrophes to show possession. Rewrite the passage putting the apostrophes in the correct places.

> Johns mother told him not to go to Peters house at all during the weeks holiday. However, while she was at work, he borrowed his brothers bike and went straight there. There was no one in, though the younger childrens toys were still out on the lawn. Peters window was open and John climbed in through it, intending to wait for him. Unfortunately for John, he was spotted by the neighbours dog and then by the neighbour…

Check your answers with a partner.

Punctuation 4
Inverted commas

This is your straightforward guide on how to use inverted commas correctly. Inverted commas are also sometimes referred to as speech marks or quotation marks. Most punctuation marks sit on the line of the page. Inverted commas hang in the air. They can be single, or double.

| 'single inverted commas' | "double inverted commas" |

There are two main times when inverted commas are used:

When a writer uses a speaker's actual words — "Good morning," he said.

When a writer is quoting from another text — The recipe says, 'Now stir in the spices.'

You are now going to look at each of these in turn.

When a writer uses a speaker's actual words

Study the use of inverted commas in the following very short story and work out the correct answers to the multiple-choice questions that follow it:

What's Wunce?

"Once," began the teacher.
"What's wunce?" asked the little girl.
"Once," repeated the teacher.
"Can you eat it?"
"Listen!" said the teacher. "Once upon …"
"What's a pon?" asked the little girl.
"Upon," repeated the teacher.
"Can you play with it?"
"Listen!" said the teacher. "Once upon … a time."
"A-time," said the little girl. "B-time. C-time. Words are so strange."

1. Each piece of speech begins and ends with:
    a a capital letter
    b inverted commas
    c a question.

2. When there is a new speaker, the writer:
    a leaves a line out
    b starts a new line
    c continues writing on the same line.

3. Every new piece of speech starts with:
    a a capital letter
    b a new line
    c an exclamation.

4. Every piece of speech is followed by:
    a a question mark
    b an exclamation mark
    c a punctuation mark.

Punctuation 4 Inverted commas

When a writer is quoting from another text

Study the use of inverted commas in the writing about this advert.

5 a Read the following advert for Benidorm Holidays.

b Now study this extract from a student's writing about the advertisement. The annotations help you to understand how to correctly quote from a text.

Benidorm holidays

Benidorm prices start from £99 for seven nights!

Benidorm, located on the Costa Blanca on the east coast of Spain, is the largest and liveliest resort in the area, attracting a million British visitors every year. Although tourism has taken away a lot of the resort's Spanish identity, Benidorm still offers everything that tourists require on a package holiday and is blessed with fantastic sandy beaches, an amazing array of entertainment and a wealth of accommodation choices. Benidorm continues to be a favourite with all types of holidaymakers, from the young 18–30 crowd lured by the prospect of the pulsating all-night clubs and discos, to the pensioners who come to enjoy the wonderful climate during the winter months and families who appreciate the great beaches and convenient facilities.

According to the advert, Benidorm is the 'largest and liveliest resort' in the area.**1** It is claimed that Benidorm offers a wide range of attractions from the 'fantastic sandy beaches' to the 'pulsating all-night clubs and discos'.**2** The wide appeal of Benidorm is shown by the reference to its 'million' visitors from Britain each year.**3** It would seem that many Britons agree that: Benidorm 'still offers everything that tourists require on a package holiday'.**4**

1 Quotation marks are placed before and after the words taken from the advert.

2 More than one quotation can be used in the same sentence.

3 A quotation can be used to give emphasis to a particular word or phrase.

4 A colon can be used to introduce a longer quotation.

---

6 Copy the following passage, which is also about the advertisement. Add inverted commas and a colon where needed. Use the rules outlined in the annotations above to help you.

According to the advert, tourism is responsible for the loss of much of the resort's Spanish identity. Nevertheless, it is still very popular with its amazing array of entertainment and its convenient facilities. Young people, in particular, are lured there by the fantastic nightlife. It would appear from the advert that none of the place's appeal has been lost. Benidorm continues to be a favourite with all types of holidaymakers.

Checkpoint

Check your answers to question 6 with a partner. Where you have different answers, use the annotations above to help you decide who is correct.

Using what you have learned from this unit, write five or six rules about the use of inverted commas to keep for reference.

131

Spelling 1
Syllables

A syllable is a unit of sound.

- A word might contain one syllable:

1
mud

- or many syllables:

1 2 3 4	1 2 3 4
en/ter/tain/ment	po/lit/i/cal

Breaking a word into syllables and sounding each syllable aloud will help you spell the word correctly. For example, saying the word dif/fi/cult aloud reminds you of the letter 'i' in the middle.

1 Copy the following words. Break them into syllables, using a forward slash (/) and numbers as shown above. Say them aloud to make sure you have identified the syllables correctly.

absolutely	possible	chocolate
prejudice	interesting	different

2 Ask a partner to test you on spelling the six words above, without looking at them.

3 In the box below there are six words that are often misspelt. Use the 'Look, Say, Cover, Write, Check' strategy to help you learn the correct spellings.

necessary	approximately	beautiful
miserable	reversible	parliament

LEARN

If you got any wrong, try this strategy:

Look at the correct spelling of the word.

Say the word by breaking it into separate syllables.

Cover the word.

Write it on a piece of paper.

Check that you have got it right.

4 Ask a partner to test you on spelling the six words above, without looking at them. Say them out loud to identify the syllables to help you.

5 a Use a dictionary to help you identify six words you think are difficult to spell. Copy them correctly.
   b Sound the words aloud and use the 'Look, Say, Cover, Write, Check' strategy to help you learn them.
   c Swap your words with a partner and test each other on them.

Spelling 2
Suffixes and prefixes

- A suffix is a letter or group of letters added to the end of a root word, which changes the meaning of the word.
- A prefix is a group of letters added to the beginning of a word to change its meaning.

Suffixes

Some frequently used suffixes are:

| -ly | -able | -ed | -ful | -ing | -ment | -ness | -ity |

In most cases you simply add the suffix to the root word, for example:

spend → spend**ing**   care → care**ful**   appoint → appoint**ment**

Sometimes you can add two suffixes to a word, for example, carefulness. If you add 'able' + 'ly' to a word, you need to drop the 'e', for example, 'honourably'.

1 Look again at the commonly used suffixes above. What new words can you make from the following words by adding one or more suffixes to them?

| wonder | reason | dread | favour | astonish |

LEARN

There are some exceptions you need to learn. Learn each of the following four rules in turn before doing the 'quick test' exercise alongside each.

RULE 1

If the word ends in a *c*, add *k* when you add a suffix beginning with *e*, *i* or *y*

For example:

picni*c* → picnic*k*ed

If the suffix does not start with *e*, *i*, or *y* do not add *k*.

QUICK TEST

Add the suffix *-ing* to the following words:
panic   traffic   picnic

Add the suffix *-al* to the following words:
magic   logic   comic

RULE 2

When adding the suffixes *-ful* or *-ly* to words that end in a consonant followed by *y*, change the *y* to *i*.

For example:

plent*y* → plent*i*ful   happ*y* → happ*i*ly

QUICK TEST

Add the suffix *-ful* to the following words:
bounty   play   beauty

English: The Basic Skills

RULE 3

When a suffix begins with a *vowel* or a *y* and the root word ends in *e*, drop the *e*.

For example: writ*e* ⟶ writ*ing*   eas*e* ⟶ eas*y*   fam*e* ⟶ fam*ous*

There are some exceptions. These are:
When the root word ends in *ee*, *oe* or *ye*, you keep the final *e*.

For example: agr*ee* ⟶ agr*eeable*   can*oe* ⟶ can*oeing*

When you add the suffix *able* to a root word that ends in *ce* or *ge* you keep the final *e*.

For example: notic*e* ⟶ notic*eable*   chang*e* ⟶ chang*eable*

QUICK TEST

Add the suffix *-ing* to the following words:
make   slow   date
guarantee   slice   type
stand

Add the suffix *-able* to the following words:
challenge   balance
debate   pronounce

RULE 4

Consonants are sometimes doubled when you add *-ar*, *-er*, *-ed* or *-ing* to a word that has one syllable and ends with a short vowel and any consonant except *y* or *x*.

For example: ru*n* ⟶ ru*nning*   hi*t* ⟶ hi*tting*
              be*g* ⟶ be*ggar*   ro*b* ⟶ ro*bber*

If the word ends in *y* or *x* do not double the consonant.

For example: pla*y* ⟶ pla*ying*   ta*x* ⟶ ta*xed*

QUICK TEST

Add the suffix *-ed* to the following words:
bar   sob   fax   tan   net

Add the suffix *-ing* to the following words:
sit   tap   set   say
put   let

Checkpoint

Check your answers to the Quick Tests with a partner. If you have different answers check to see who is correct and make any necessary changes. Use a dictionary if you are not sure.

Prefixes

Remember, a prefix is a group of letters added to the beginning of a word to change its meaning.

spell ⟶ **mis**spell   appear ⟶ **dis**appear   happy ⟶ **un**happy

2 Some of the most common prefixes are listed in the first column on the next page. Match them to the base words in the second column to make new words. Some base words work with more than one prefix e.g. *dis*appear, *re*appear. The base words are in groups of ten. Work through one group before moving on to the next. See how many new words you can form in five minutes.

Spelling 2 Suffixes and prefixes

Prefixes	Base words

re
mis
in
sub
im
anti
ir
dis
un
	a behave place trust order honest
	   like organise obedient responsible kind
	
	b social clockwise aware able conscious
	   healthy fortunate form insure produce
	
	c effective equality secure proper material
	   polite possible rational regular standard

Combining prefixes and suffixes

Knowing how to use and spell prefixes and suffixes correctly gives you access to a whole new range of words. For example:

success	honest	satisfy
successful	honesty	satisfied
successfully	honestly	satisfying
unsuccessful	dishonest	satisfiable
unsuccessfully	dishonesty	satisfaction
	dishonestly	satisfactory
		satisfyingly
		unsatisfied
		dissatisfy
		dissatisfying
		unsatisfactory

3 Using the chart on the right, make as many words as you can using the root words, a prefix and one or more suffixes. Use the spelling rules you have learned to help you spell all your words correctly.

Prefixes	Root words	Suffixes
re	agree	able
mis		ment
in	fair	ly
sub		ed
im	reverse	ful
de		ing
ir	sense	ion
dis		ible
un	perfect	less
	skill	

135

Spelling 3
Plurals

Plural means more than one.

Rules for making plurals

For most plural forms you simply add **s** to the singular forms.

For example:　　book ⟶ book**s**　　computer ⟶ computer**s**

There are a few exceptions. You need to learn these. Learn the rules in the first Learn box.

QUICK TEST

Using the rules, write the plurals of the following words.

a branch　Christmas　beach　fear　atlas　inch
　circus　change　blush　speech　hoax　girl　witch
　bonus　plus　gas　laugh　arch　coach　head
　dish　blotch　week

b holiday　casualty　essay　convoy　lady　joy
　comedy　melody　remedy　study　bully　delay　key
　county　anniversary　takeaway　berry　gallery

LEARN 1

- When the singular form ends in -*s*, -*x*, -*ch* or -*sh*, add -*es*:
  bus ⟶ bus**es**
  tax ⟶ tax**es**
  church ⟶ church**es**
  flash ⟶ flash**es**
- If a word ends in -*y* and has a consonant before the last letter change the *y* to an *i* and add *es*:
  party ⟶ part**ies**

There are some other exceptions to the rules. Learn the examples given in the second Learn box and the following irregular plurals.

Irregular plurals

There are a number of irregular plurals in the English language. These words do not follow the usual rules for making plurals.

You will know some of them:
child ⟶ children　　man ⟶ men　　sheep ⟶ sheep
mouse ⟶ mice　　tooth ⟶ teeth　　deer ⟶ deer

Others may not be so familiar to you such as:
formula ⟶ formulae　　　stimulus ⟶ stimuli
crisis ⟶ crises　　　　emphasis ⟶ emphases

Keep a record of any unusual plurals you come across, so that you will know how to spell them in your own writing.

Checkpoint

Write the plurals of the following words. Use a dictionary to check your answers.

　　dash　crunch　disc　trolley　woman　ox
　　proof　baby　life　axis　domino　fax　screen
　　half　spy　lunch　belief　desk　wife

LEARN 2

- If a word ends in -*o* you usually just add *s*. However, there are a few commonly used words that need *es* to make them plural
  tomat**o** ⟶ tomat**oes**
  potat**o** ⟶ potat**oes**
  hero ⟶ her**oes**
- If a word ends in -*f* or -*fe* you usually change the -*f* or -*fe* to -*ves*:
  wolf ⟶ wolves
  knife ⟶ knives.

But there are a few exceptions:
roo**f** ⟶ roo**fs**
chie**f** ⟶ chie**fs**
ree**f** ⟶ ree**fs**

Spelling 4
Homonyms

■ Homonyms are words which have the same spelling or pronunciation as another, but a different meaning or origin.

Types of homonym

There are two different kinds of homonym:
- Words which have the same *spelling* as another but a different meaning. The pronunciation may be the same, for example:

    | calf | calf |

    or different, for example:

    | lead | lead |

- Words which have the same *sound* as another but different meaning or different spelling, for example:

    | read/reed | pair/pear |

This is the most common type.

People sometimes get confused over which spelling they should use. You need to be extra careful to make sure you have the correct word and spelling when using a computer spellchecker. It will only tell you if you have an incorrect spelling, not if you have chosen the wrong word.

1. Each of the following sentences contains three homonyms used incorrectly. Rewrite the sentences using the correct words.
    a He mist the ball and new he had throne away the game.
    b She new the bred was in the kitchen but she couldn't fined it.
    c He walked passed the lane on his write and turned towards the would.

2. The words below are all homonyms. Copy them and next to each one write one word that sounds the same but is spelt differently.

    | sea | pour | great | rowed | way | piece | profit | soul |
    | lone | pair | hole | hare | hymn | ate | allowed| ceiling |
    | new | raise | teas | you | | | | |

Checkpoint
Check your answers to question 2 with a partner. Where you have differences, use a dictionary to check who is correct.

3. Choose five pairs of words that are homonyms. You could use some of the examples above or new words of your own. For each pair, write a sentence which uses both words correctly.

Spelling 5
Using a dictionary

A dictionary is a very useful tool. It helps you to:

- find the meaning of a word you do not know
- pronounce the word correctly
- spell the word correctly.

For example:

> correct spelling ⟶ community (say k'mewni-tee) ⟵ pronunciation noun
> any group living in one place or having common interests. ⟵ meaning

© Pearson Education

You are allowed to use a dictionary in your Functional English tests.

How a dictionary is organised

A dictionary is organised in alphabetical order. All the words that start with the letter *a* are grouped together followed by all the words that start with the letter *b*, and so on through the alphabet.

It is not just the first letter of the word that counts. When you have several words starting with the same two, three or even more letters, you have to go further into each word to find its alphabetical order.

1 a Place the following groups of words in alphabetical order:

> drastic icing best public free money risk envelope trial silver
> ready rush rattle reason ring robot range roller rider red
> grief grind grit grill grime grid grizzly grin grip grievance

b Check your answers with another student. Where you have different answers, use a dictionary to check who is correct.

How to find the right page in a dictionary

When you want to find a particular word you should look at the words in bold at the top of the pages. These are the first and last words on that page. They are called guide words. If the word you are looking for comes between these two words alphabetically, you are on the correct page.

2 Here are four words and below them the guide words from four pages in a dictionary. Which page would you turn to to find each word?

> skull   skate   skyscraper   skill

Page 966	sixteen	sketch
Page 967	skew	skint
Page 968	skin-tight	skylark
Page 969	skylight	slap

Spelling 5 **Using a dictionary**

How to find the correct spelling

It's more difficult to find a word if you don't know how to spell it. But all you really need to do is use what you know about words and letter combinations to make an intelligent guess. You might not know how to spell the word poltergeist, but by saying the word aloud you would be able to work out the first three or four letters – enough to enable you to find it in the dictionary.

3 In the words that follow, some letters have been missed out. Use your dictionary and some intelligent guesses to help you work out what the words are.

| pri_i_ege | mo_aster_ | sa_dwic_ |
| mac_in__y | ass_g_ment | bis__it |

Some words start with a silent letter. Silent letters are letters you can't hear when you say the word but are there when you need to write it, for example, knife.

4 In each of the following words, the first letter is silent. Work out what the letter should be and write the word in full:

_riting   _nitting   _nome   _sychiatry   _nuckle

_naw   _sychological   _restle   _now   _narl

The more you practise using a dictionary, the quicker you will become. You can use a dictionary in your Functional English tests to:

- find the meaning of a word you do not know
- check the meaning of a word you want to use
- check the spelling of a word you want to use.

5 Find and write down the meanings of the following words as quickly as you can.

diminutive   collate   ruminate   epilogue   posthumous   accrue

6 The following words are spelled incorrectly. Correct them using your dictionary to help you.

earing   restaraunt   absenteism   tomohawk   conscus   tonsallitis

139

English: The Basic Skills

Acknowledgements

The publisher would like to thank copyright holders for permission to reproduce the following material.

Text

Page 12: information about Connexions reprinted with kind permission; pp 15 and 17: article 'Kellogg, the global breakfast cereal company …' from *The Independent*, 25th October 2006. Reprinted with permission; p15: extract from *Insight Guide: Caribbean, the Lesser Antilles* p261 published by Insight Guides/Berlitz Publishing. Reprinted with permission; p18 'Keirin' extract from www.wikipedia.org; p30: article 'I feel a right Charlie' copyright © *Daily Mail* 23 October 2007 by Luke Salkeld. Photo copyright © SWNS reprinted with permission; p34: extract of text from www.Newcastle Gateshead.com reprinted with permission of NewcastleGateshead Initiative. Photograph © Graeme Peacock. Reprinted with permission of Graeme Peacock; text and photograph from www.yha.org.uk. Reprinted with permission of YHA (England and Wales) Limited; p35: text and photograph of Ragdale Hall reprinted with kind permission of Ragdale Hall Health Hydro; text about Benidorm from www.directlineholidays.co.uk. Reprinted with permission of Direct Line Holidays; text from www.outdooradventure.co.uk. Reprinted with permission; p38: 'Best of New York City' 3rd Edition, Ginger Adams Otis, Lonely Planet Publications 2005, pp 8-9. Copyright © 2005 Lonely Planet Publications. Reprinted with permission; p40: use of extract from TV Listing *The Guardian Guide* 14-20 October 2006. Copyright © The Press Association. Reprinted with permission; extract from a York-Newcastle train timetable North and Southbound, including keys. Copyright © GNER. Please note these times were correct at time of going to print but are changed on a regular basis. Reprinted with kind permission of GNER; p42: use of map of Louth, graphs and text extracts from LOUTH, by Lorna Blackwood, *The Times*, 10 August 2007. Copyright © Lorna Blackwood, NI Syndication Ltd, 10 August 2007. Used with permission; p54: extract from Director General's Report BBC. Copyright © BBC. Reprinted with permission; report by police constable Thomas Stock of an incident at the public house on 18th April 1875 copyright © Hooper and Fletcher archive; extract from example of a homebuyer's report from www.TheMoveChannel.com copyright © TheMoveChannel. Reprinted with kind permission; p57: use of an AA report on the Mini Cooper, from www.theaa.com. copyright © The AA. Reprinted with permission; p60: use of text, one line drawing and front cover illustration from Mike Hattan's sports massage leaflet. Copyright © Mike Hattan. Reproduced with kind permission of the author; pp 62-65: extracts from DVLA form D1 and booklet INF1D reprinted with the kind permission of the DVLA. Please note the PDFs and application forms are constantly being updated. Updated information can be found on the DVLA website; p70: 'For your safety and comfort' from airline in-flight magazine copyright © Jet2.com. Reprinted with permission; p79: 'The Teenage Blog Outbreak' by Ken Snodin from www.content-articles.com; p83: extract adapted from 'You did it, son', Steven Morris, *The Guardian*, 4th January

2007. Reprinted with permission; pp84-85: use of text based on TV programme 'Fortune: Million Pound Giveaway' and logo copyright © Fever Media, reprinted with kind permission; p86: 'The York Dungeon' leaflet copyright © Merlin Entertainments. Reprinted with permission; p90: article 'Stone me! Masons in prize swoop' copyright © The Press, 11th October 2007. Reprinted with permission; p93: Science report copyright © Deirdre Keating. Reprinted with permission; p96: use of an extract from a Tourism Ireland direct mail leaflet. Reprinted with permission; p98: PhotoPlus 7 advertisement copyright © Serif (Europe) Limited 2007 www.serif.com. Reprinted with permission; p100: article about Jigsaw copyright © words by Melanie Rickey/Grazia. Reprinted with permission; p102: extract 'Radio days are here again as Britons tune, click and plug into digital age' from *The Guardian* 17th August 2008, John Plunkett. Reprinted with permission; pp 104-105: extracts by Katie Allen, *The Guardian* 23 August, 2007. Copyright © Guardian News and Media 2007. Reprinted with permission; p110: article 'Wild Thoughts' by Mark Carwardine from *BBC Wildlife Magazine*, April 2006. Reprinted with permission of *BBC Wildlife Magazine*; p113: use of short extract from 'Whaling Agency Faces a Possible Shift' by Juliet Eilperin, Staff Writer, The Washington Post, 2nd June 2006. Reprinted with permission; short extract from 'The Slaughter of Animals for Food' by Dr. Harold Hillman Mb BSc PhD. Copyright © Harold Hillman. Reprinted with kind permission of the author; pp118-119: extracts adapted from www.dooy-oo.co.uk/discussions/would-you-ever-wear-fur/1035600/; short extract 'I was browsing the new topics and this one caught my eye ...' reprinted with the kind permission of the author; 'Top 10 reasons for wearing fur' copyright © Fur Council of Canada, for further details see www.furcouncil.com, reprinted with permission; p124: extract from www.actionaid.org. Reprinted with the kind permission of ActionAid; p125: extract about leeches from *BBC Wildlife Magazine*, April 2006. Reprinted with permission of *BBC Wildlife Magazine*; p131: text about Benidorm from www.directlineholidays.co.uk. Reprinted with permission of Direct Line Holidays; p138: use of one definition from *Heinemann English Dictionary*. Copyright © Pearson Education, Australia. Reprinted with kind permission of the publisher.

Photographs

Page 4: Young man sitting in front of computer screen with webcam (42-15475295 RM) © Freitag/zefa/Corbis; Teenager writing at desk (EDU16) © BananaStock Education (NT); Teenagers talking (A252BK) © Alamy/Jim West; p5: Interview © Getty images; Office worker (4773449) © iStock; Mother with son on knees (A129CN) © Pegaz/Alamy; Teenager at desk (EDU17) © BananaStock Education (NT); Male student in library (3567459) © iStock; p6: Facebook and Friends Reunited logos reproduced with permission; p7: Girls bowling (3300856) © iStock; Teenage boy playing guitar (5430890) © iStock; p9: Food service employee (4426738) © iStock; Care assistant © Photofusion Picture Library/Alamy; Office worker (4773449) © iStock; p11: Teenager talking to parent (ADM0C5) © Alamy/Laura Dwight; p13: Business woman © Photodisc 73 (NT); p15 Cereal boxes © Stockbyte (NT); Children on a beach © Photodisc 71 (NT); Cricket players (AD7A0F)

© Alamy/Robert Harding Picture Library; p16: School lunch (A2RKX1) © Alamy/Adrian Sherratt; p18: Cyclist © Digital Vision 11 (NT); p19: Cyclist © Digital Vision 11 (NT); p20: Guitarist © Image 100 Teenagers (NT); Teenagers building path in wildlife garden, UK (ACEF5F) © Photofusion Picture Library/Alamy; Footballers © Digital Vision 12 (NT); Fashion model © Corel 672 (NT); p24: Group of teenagers (TEEN 95) © BananaStock Teenagers (NT); p27: London photo © 015LON (NT); p30: Charlie Thomas © SWNS: p34: Photo from NewcastleGateshead extract © Graeme Peacock. Reprinted with permission of Graeme Peacock; YHA Keswick from www.yha.org.uk. Reprinted with permission of YHA (England and Wales) Limited; Photograph of Ragdale Hall reprinted with kind permission of Ragdale Hall Health Hydro; Benidorm (3223962) © iStock; Widemouth Bay, Cornwall (AJEE3N) © Mark Dyball/Alamy; p39: use of two images of the Statue of Liberty © Lonely Planet Images. Reprinted with permission; p44: Apartment block (3818223) © iStock; Terraced housing (4328106) © iStock; p45: Padstow Harbour (2222463) © iStock; p46: Burger © Ingram Ultimate Food Photograph; p47: Burger close-up © Ingram Ultimate Food Photography; p48: Chef dressing plates (A0HJTD) © Alamy/ImageState; p53: Woman on phone (2155687) © iStock; Mother with son on knees (A129CN) © Pegaz/Alamy; Middle-aged man on phone (AGMGNE) © Corbis Super RF/Alamy; Young man talking on phone (5093186) © iStock; p57: Mini Cooper with the permission of The AA; p58: Swimming pool (4427113) © iStock; p60: Sports therapist (2274275) © iStock; p61: Tennis player (5095110) © iStock; Hockey player (1892872) © iStock; Cricket player (901312) © iStock; p63: Young woman learner driver looking in her wing mirror (AAEEBW) © Angela Hampton Picture Library/Alamy; p65: Teenager at desk (EDU17) © BananaStock Education (NT); p68: Young businessman in office (AX4J1D) © WoodyStock/Alamy; p78: Young man sitting in front of computer screen with webcam (42-15475295 RM) © Freitag/zefa/Corbis; p79: Girl typing on computer keyboard (AX065576 RM) © Rick Gomez/CORBIS; p80: Couple at computer (ABB4D8 RF) © Image Source Pink/Alamy; p82: Young girl © Stockbyte 19 (NT); Worried businessman and Woman on telephone © Ingram Diamond Volume 1 CD 1 (NT); Amazed woman © Ingram 500 CD 1(NT); Woman with laptop © Ingram Platinum Volume 2 CD 6 (NT); Beaming smile Botswanian man © Gary Cook/Alamy; Eyes and hands © Photodisc 2 (NT); p83: Michael and Peter Perham © Michael Perham; p90: Stone carver at work (ACC1C6) © DigitalVues/Alamy; p97: Beach (2180403) © iStock; Paddington Station (1103522) © iStock; p98: Advertising office (5476303) © iStock; p99: Compass (5057518) © iStock; Mobile phone (5395519) © iStock; Digital camera (3656965) © iStock; MP3 player (4282118) © iStock; p100: Jigsaw store (ACMBDD) © Yadid Levy/Alamy; p101: Jogging shoes (3333212) © iStock; Fashion store (29112550) © iStock; Video game controller (3106657); p102: MP3 player (5371295) © iStock; p103: Radio (4644592) © iStock; Woman listening to music on laptop (5494941) © iStock; Podcast icon (4960578) © iStock; WiFi icon (4960891) © iStock; p106: Traffic queuing in a town high street © Stan Gamester/Alamy; p108: Waste bin © Photodisc 31 (NT); A group of teenage boys and girls sitting in a shopping arcade © Adrian Sherratt/Alamy: p110: Whale © Digital Vision (NT); Attempts to rescue the whale © Getty

Images/Peter Macdiarmid; River Thames © Digital Vision (NT); p114: L-plates (3567656) © iStock; p115: Person writing in notebook (3584474) © iStock; p118: Woman in long fur coat © Corel 672 (NT); p119-121: Woman in knee-length fur coat © Ingram 500 CD 1 (NT); Model © Corel 738 (NT); Maple leaves © Photodisc 38B (NT); p123: Eskimo © Corel 11 (NT); White fox © Digital Vision Animal Faces (NT); p125: Leeches © Science Photo Library/Martin Dohrn.